SCHOOL-BASED PRACTICE WITH C
YOUTH EXPERIENCING HOMEL

D0864864

SCHOOL-BASED PRACTICE WITH CHILDREN AND YOUTH EXPERIENCING HOMELESSNESS

James P. Canfield

OXFORD WORKSHOP SERIES

OXFORD
UNIVERSITY PRESS

OXFORD
UNIVERSITY PRESS

Oxford University Press is a department of the University of
Oxford. It furthers the University's objective of excellence in research,
scholarship, and education by publishing worldwide.

Oxford   New York
Auckland   Cape Town   Dar es Salaam   Hong Kong   Karachi
Kuala Lumpur   Madrid   Melbourne   Mexico City   Nairobi
New Delhi   Shanghai   Taipei   Toronto

With offices in
Argentina   Austria   Brazil   Chile   Czech Republic   France   Greece
Guatemala   Hungary   Italy   Japan   Poland   Portugal   Singapore
South Korea   Switzerland   Thailand   Turkey   Ukraine   Vietnam

Oxford is a registered trademark of Oxford University Press
in the UK and certain other countries.

Published in the United States of America by
Oxford University Press
198 Madison Avenue, New York, NY 10016

Library of Congress Cataloging-in-Publication Data
Canfield, James P. (James Park)
School-based practice with children and youth experiencing homelessness
/ by James P. Canfield.
pages cm. — (School Social Work Association of America (SSWAA)
Oxford workshop series)
Includes bibliographical references and index.
ISBN 978–0–19–021305–3 (alk. paper)
1. Homeless children—United States.   2. Homeless youth—United States.
3. Social service—United States.   I. Title.
HV4505.C33 2015
371.7086′9420973—dc23
2014043049

1 3 5 7 9 8 6 4 2
Printed in the United States of America
on acid-free paper

I dedicate this book to anyone and everyone who has
ever helped me directly or indirectly.

Contents

Preface

I really enjoy going to the School Social Work Association of America (SSWAA) Annual Conference. It is always a great opportunity to see old friends and colleagues and meet new ones. What I really like about the conference is that it gives me, a researcher, an opportunity to remain grounded. I love talking to practitioners because I find they provide the greatest insight into where I can direct my research focus and hopefully provide meaningful findings. When I first started going to the Conference, I would run into people who served as designated homeless liaisons. These were people in federally mandated positions who are assigned to work with homeless children and youth, and it seemed like these were the folks who mainly dealt with homelessness as part of their school-based practice. Now when I go to the Conference, so many more school social workers are contending with the impact of homelessness on outcomes both directly and indirectly.

This mirrors the current trend facing many communities in America. Financial instability and austerity measures taken by the United States are expected to increase the number of children and families experiencing homelessness tremendously. Currently, an estimated 920,000 to 1,400,000 children and families experience homelessness in a given year (National Coalition for the Homeless, 2009). However, these numbers were calculated based on the number of children and families that request services, drastically underestimating the actual number of families with children who experience homelessness in a given year. Our nation's schools are continually contending with the large and growing number of students experiencing homelessness and in need of services. Unfortunately, the amount of homeless children has outpaced the amount of funding and services available to serve these students.

School social workers are often at the forefront in facilitating services to these students, usually through the provisions of the McKinney-Vento Homeless Assistance Act (MVA). The MVA requires education agencies to employ liaisons to serve as gatekeepers to education for homeless children and youth—a role that usually falls to a school social worker. These practitioners in particular play an important role in the lives of homeless students; however, school social workers as a whole need a basic understanding of the impact of homelessness and the policy provisions that are designed to address it. As we understand more and more that factors outside of the school greatly impact the education of our youth, homelessness will become a major focus and issue for the profession. This volume in the SSWAA Oxford Workshop Series was written to provide a guide to school-based practice with homeless children and youth. The volume discusses how we should approach homelessness in our practice. We will discuss how we should use an ecological-systems perspective to give us a broad conceptualization of homelessness. Along these lines, we should view homelessness as an experience with many different systems that can impact an outcome. We should approach the issue by examining the different systems inherent to an experience of homelessness that serve as barriers or facilitators to an outcome and our practice. This volume offers a general guide to the provisions of the MVA, which provides the backbone to our practice with homeless children and youth.

This volume also presents a condensed guide to the literature on homelessness. There are a multitude of studies on child homelessness, enough to make reviewing the knowledge base very difficult and unwieldy. Therefore this volume focuses on providing the information relevant to school-based practitioners. Going over the pertinent literature on children and youth experiencing homelessness will provide a solid background and foundation on the topic. This volume takes time to give a comprehensive review of the important (to school-based practitioners) provisions in federal policy followed by a review of the literature on the MVA and its implications for practice. Finally, we will discuss a practice mindset for practicing with homeless children and youth in school settings. Importantly, we will discuss what can be done to address barriers to educational opportunities that homeless children face.

Acknowledgments

I would like to acknowledge James J. Canfield, Kil Cha Canfield, Daniel Canfield, Dana Harley, Willie Elliott, Vanessa Hunn, Megan Lindsey, and Lori Mangan for their help in reviewing the manuscript. I would also like to acknowledge Agnes Bannigan for helping me through this whole process and Brianna Marron for helping me get to the finish line. I would like to also acknowledge Kevin Eastman in giving me encouragement to pursue writing. It goes to show how a little support, even in very brief interactions between total strangers, can go a long way. I would like to specifically acknowledge Ramin Mohajer for his support in organizing and conceptualizing the book. I would like to recognize my mentor and role model, Dr. Martell L. Teasley for helping me bring this book to fruition, helping me organize and conceptualize the book, and more importantly, putting me in a position to even write this book. Finally, I would like to acknowledge my family: Payton "Peety" Hodge's smiles kept me going when things were tough. I need to especially thank Sabrina A. Canfield for everything she has done for me, and putting up with the long hours needed to complete this manuscript. She is the best.

I

Who Are the Homeless?

Two twin girls, about eight years old, sat in the disheveled waiting room of a local homeless coalition. Old magazines and colored-in coloring books were strewn about the room like unraked leaves on a drafty fall morning. Their parents were the last to see the Reverend, an affable and hard-working man whose meetings held the hope of referrals and donations. This was the end of "walk-in" day, wherein people experiencing homelessness could come into the homeless coalition without an appointment for help. The two girls waited for their parents by watching the very, very end of *Finding Nemo* (the aforementioned Nemo had been found and reunited with his father at this point). Their contented affect contrasted the forlorn look the people who usually occupied those seats wore, but hinted at their comfort in these types of waiting rooms and situations.

The two girls watched the movie through the credits, reading each line as a condemned prisoner reading his last words—holding on for any extra seconds of life and enjoyment. Like a guillotine blade falling, the movie returned to the DVD menu screen and the girls would need an adult to restart the movie. They approached the MSW intern entrusted to oversee and organize "walk-in" day and asked him if he could restart the movie. The intern was good-natured and hard-working, but a little naïve—he was barely old enough to legally order a drink, but did really well in his social work studies. He looked for where the secretary (who was out that day) kept the remote, but could not find it. Finally, he went up to the DVD player and tried pressing the buttons but with no luck. The two girls, accustomed to defeat and futility when solutions were so close, said, "It's OK. Thanks," and made a familiar, weighted trudge to their seats. The MSW intern, who genuinely felt bad he couldn't help, went back to keeping order to the "walk-in" day that would be over once the girls' parents left their meeting.

The girls ached for something to do—all of the crayons were in a Ziploc bag and were that purplish gray color that happens to all old crayons stuffed together in a bag. But even if they had a wide selection of colors, and brand new pointy crayons, they had nothing to color in. So as kids do, they began to explore the room.

In a moment of keen awareness, the young intern intercepted the girls before they got to the expensive copy machine not-for-profits such as this protected with the fierceness of a Viking raid. He offered to come up with an activity. He asked them, "Do you guys want to play a game? Do you guys want to play hangman?"

The twins lit up and said in that eerie unison only twins can produce, "Can we play scrambles?"

"What's that?"

"It's our favorite. It's those games where you unscramble letters to make words!" they said sped through in perfect harmony.

So the three played scrambles. The intern started with easy words like "ball" and "ship" which soon gave way to harder words like "basketball" and "cruise." The girls were so good at this game they would often unscramble the letters into words before the intern finished writing all of the letters on the sheet of paper. Finally, in perfect union, they wanted "a really, really, really, really, really hard one." So the intern scrambled "zygomorphic."

He went back to overseeing the empty waiting room while the girls got to work. After about five minutes, they brought the paper to the intern and asked him if this was the right word. He started to reply "well its clo . . ." but his jaw went off a cliff like a coyote chasing a roadrunner before he finished what he was about to say. They had unscrambled it. The two twin girls sitting in the waiting room of a local homeless coalition had unscrambled the word "zygomorphic," a word the intern only knew because of studying for the GRE a year earlier.

"How . . .? How did you figure this out?" asked the intern in a surprised but genuine and honest way that respected the obvious intelligence in front of him.

"Well, we knew morph was a word, *ic* usually comes at the end, *g* and *z* won't go next to each other, so it was this or gyzomorphic," they explained to the intern, "we guessed it was zygomorphic. What does it mean?"

"I, uh, don't really, uh remember . . ." the intern stammered trying to hide his embarrassment.

"Can we look it up?"

So the three looked up the word zygomorphic (it means something can be cut in a way so that the two halves are mirror images) and began just talking. And their genius unfolded. They spoke like adults, but not in a parentified way, just in a calm confidence, especially about reading. They read every Ramona book in the library and were impressed by the intern's memory of *Ramona the Brave*. The intern then asked what he thought was an innocuous question, "What do you want to be when you grow up?" expecting the "usual" responses: teacher, doctor, police officer, Beyonce.

The two girls responded without hesitation, "a worker."

"Like a social worker?" the intern asked, beaming with professional pride. We *make* a difference he thought.

"No, like one at Winn Dixie (a grocery store)," one of the twins said.

"No, Lowes (a hardware store) would be better, they pay more," the other eight-year-old twin corrected her sister, "yeah that would be good."

"Wait, you guys don't want to be doctors or lawyers or teachers?!? You guys are so smart; you could be whatever you want! Anything you want!"

"Wait. We could be teachers or doctors? Really? No we can't," they said as they dropkicked the intern's heart into his conscience.

"Wait, why . . . why not?"

Like a little leaguer striking out swinging returning to an overbearing coach, they quickly shrugged, "Ahdonknow."

The intern was always at the top of his class, but all of the schooling and "A" papers he wrote did not give him a prescribed answer to this situation. So he spoke honestly from that area of the brain that takes over when one needs to say something with absolute belief, "Listen to me; you girls are the smartest people I have ever met. You girls are so smart that whatever you really want to be, you will be it. Thank you for talking to me."

Before the girls could respond, their parents stepped out of the Reverend's office. They where hunched over wearing the weight of disappointment yet again. "Girls! We need to get going! Now!" the Mom firmly told her daughters. They dutifully and abruptly packed up and said a quick and smiley "bye" to the intern and left through the door, most likely to wait in line at the family shelter a couple of miles away.

* * *

I never found out what happened to those two girls. That experience is the reason why I research and work with homeless children and youth. All children at the very least deserve hope, and to hear those bright and intelligent kids tell me that their childhood dream was to become a worker at a grocery store still affects me to this day. I would like to think that they grew up into highly successful people, but the reality is that like many children and youth in their situation, they face many challenges to future success. Child homelessness is a growing issue for our communities and schools. An estimated 2.3 to 3.5 million individuals experience homelessness throughout the course of a year (National Coalition for the Homeless, 2009) and 40% of these individuals are thought to be children (Urban Institute, 2000 as cited in National Coalition for the Homeless, 2009; Rukmana, 2008). These numbers do not reflect the recent housing crisis, which most likely increased the number of homeless families with children, but these estimates do not include those who do not seek services, drastically underestimating the actual count of those experiencing homelessness (National Coalition for the Homeless, 2009).

Over the last 100 years, our view of homelessness has changed from predominately single, nomadic vagabonds, bums, and hobos, or in the case of children, scamps and scallywags, to understanding that entire families can become homeless. We also understand that homelessness should be thought of as a multifaceted experience, with different factors or systems influencing a homeless individual or family's situation (Nooe & Patterson, 2010; Rafferty, Shinn, & Weitzman, 2004). Oftentimes, homelessness is an experience of transience—meaning those experiencing homelessness frequently move between different housing and homeless situations. For children and youth, transience manifests itself as unplanned school mobility (Julianelle & Foscarinis, 2003). Unexpectedly moving between schools places homeless children behind their peers in academic achievement from missing school days, possibly delaying the diagnosis of learning disabilities, and/or other problems associated with changing schools (Julianelle & Foscarinis, 2003). These problems stem from difficulties in accessing education along with other personal or familial barriers to education (Biggar,

2001; Jozefowicz-Simbeni & Israel, 2006; Julianelle & Foscarinis, 2003; Urban Institute, 2004).

We as school social workers and related-services professionals are frequently at the forefront of addressing these barriers, often through carrying out important policy provisions. This chapter will provide us with a foundation of how we should approach homelessness in our practice as school social workers and related-services professionals. We will go through different perspectives about homelessness, begin our examination of policy aspects in our practice through discussing federal definitions, and organize our thoughts on this complex issue. Finally, we will discuss using the evidence-based practice model to address homelessness in our schools.

What Is Homelessness?

Before we talk about how we can address homelessness in our schools, we should sharpen our focus by developing an understanding of what is homelessness. It is a complex issue without a conclusive, universally agreed-upon definition. However, as we will discuss a little later in the book, school-based practice with homeless children and youth often revolves around carrying out federal policy provisions, so a good place to start would be the US federal definitions of homelessness. The definitions will give us a broad and general description of what homelessness is, but more importantly, it helps us understand who is eligible for services.

Several different federal agencies address homelessness and may have their own specific definition, but we will focus on two specifically: the Department of Housing and Urban Development (HUD) and the Department of Education (DOE). Here is HUD's general definition of who is considered homeless:

> an individual who lacks a fixed, regular, and adequate nighttime residence; and an individual who has a primary nighttime residence that is: 1) a supervised publicly or privately operated shelter designed to provide temporary living accommodations (including welfare hotels, congregate shelters, and transitional housing for the mentally ill), 2) an institution that provides a temporary residence for individuals intended to be institutionalized, or 3) a public or private place not designed for, or ordinarily used as, a regular sleeping accommodation for human beings.
>
> (US Department of Housing and Urban Development, 2007)

The Department of Education uses the same basic definition, but also includes migrant farm children, foster care children, and children who are "doubled up." This means that a child lives, in a nonpermanent situation, with relatives or friends (think of "couch surfing").

There are two important aspects of the definition we should consider: first, the federal definition includes many different ways someone could be homeless. For example, someone or a family could be homeless if they are sleeping in their car, living in an abandoned building, or staying in a homeless shelter (Congressional Research Service, 2005). We will discuss the implications of this in the coming sections. And the second is the phrase: "fixed, regular, and adequate nighttime residence." This phrase will show up several times as we talk about homelessness, and as we think of homelessness, fixed, regular, and adequate are the guidelines we should follow when determining who is considered to be experiencing homelessness.

How We Think of Homelessness . . .

. . . as a Status

Often, practice and research take a de facto approach to characterizing homelessness. We often treat homelessness as a status: one either is or is not homeless. Basically, anyone fitting the definitions is considered "homeless," regardless of where they are staying (e.g., shelter, car, public park) or how they became homeless (natural disasters, domestic violence, poor economic conditions, etc.). On its face, this makes sense. Why not call the people who fit the definition of homelessness, "homeless"? However, this approach belies the complexity that experiencing homelessness is for people, especially children and youth. Nor does it take into account the unique elements that each case of homelessness contains and the subsequent repercussions of these elements on our interventions. We must recognize that there may be systematic differences in each of the various scenarios in which a child could be considered homeless. For example, a child who resides in a transitional housing program may have access to well-lit, quiet, and safe places to study, whereas a youth who is staying in a shelter may not have access to a computer to complete assignments or may not be able to concentrate because of the noise level at an emergency shelter.

Thinking of or treating homelessness as a status has confounded over 25 years of research on the subject. Buckner's 2008 systematic review assessed the body of literature on studies comparing homeless children to their impoverished, but housed peers. He found little consistency in the findings: Some studies found that homeless children had worse outcomes, whereas others found that impoverished, but housed, children suffered more (Buckner, 2008). One of his conclusions is that much of the inconsistency is because we often treat all homeless children as an aggregate, meaning we treat homelessness as a status, rather than viewing the situation as an experience.

. . . as an Experience

We should think of homelessness as an *experience*, rather than a status. The federal definition of homelessness inherently includes different situations wherein someone could be considered homeless. Each of these situations, such as sleeping in a public place or residing in a welfare motel, may offer different risks, stressors, or other factors associated with each experience. Every situation of homelessness brings with it unique circumstances and challenges that will impact practice with homeless children and youth. It is a "constellation of risk factors" that may impact a given outcome (Rafferty, Shinn, & Weitzman, 2004). Our understanding of the different elements inherent to a situation of homelessness is important to appropriately practicing with homeless children and youth.

One of those key elements of conceptualizing homelessness as an experience revolves around time. For families, the US shelter system is based on our thinking that homelessness was a temporary experience. Families were just "knocked off their feet" and just needed some time to recover. So shelters were built and intended to be the main form of support, mainly serving as a stopgap between periods of housing. However, we now understand that homelessness may be a long-term experience. And on top of this, homeless families can cycle through housing and homeless situations. Time aspects of homelessness can be generally broken up in three ways: transitional, episodic, and chronic (Hule & Culhane, 1998, cited in McAllister et al., 2010). Transitional homelessness is the traditional view of homelessness. Families who are shifting in-between housing situations are experiencing transitional homelessness, meaning families become homeless in emergency or temporary situations. Some children and families shuffle in and out of homeless situations in an episodic way. They may find safe, fixed, regular, and adequate nighttime housing for a month, then spend two months on the streets, followed by a week or two of housing, then back to the shelter for a spell, and so on. This experience is a very common one for the children and youth we serve in schools because oftentimes families do not find permanent solutions to their housing needs. Finally, the chronically homeless are those who are permanently entrenched on the streets, in shelters, or other situations of homelessness.

A Perspective on Homelessness

It can be easy to get lost in all of the different situations, circumstances, and conditions of homelessness. The previous section outlines some of the complexities in a general way, but we need a way to organize our thoughts. An easy way to do this is to adopt an ecological-systems perspective when thinking about homelessness. This perspective provides a framework for our understanding and a foundation to develop interventions. The ecological-systems perspective originally comes from biology and states that all organisms are systems, participate in super-systems, and are made up of subsystems (Payne, 2014). So for social workers and other related professions, practice should view a social problem, such as homelessness, as a collection of different factors rather than focusing on the reduced parts of an issue (Payne, 2014; Turner, 1996). So if we adopt the ecological-systems perspective, we would view homelessness as a result of the relationships between any and all of the interrelated factors that may impact a situation (Nooe & Patterson, 2010). This ranges from micro-level interpersonal factors such as addiction, mental health, or education, to larger societal components such as housing prices, job availability, and wages (Nooe & Patterson, 2010).

Our schools can be considered systems. For school social workers and related professionals, our practice setting is where the organizational focus is, not on social services, counseling, or mental health treatment. Because of this, we often contend with a multitude of different factors that may influence our practice (Allen-Meares, 2010), necessitating a need to have an understanding of how different systems can impact situations our students find themselves in as well as our practice interventions. Formal, informal, and societal systems outside of the school will impact how individuals or families become or stay homeless, or leave homelessness (Nooe & Patterson, 2010), and the different systems that make up an educational agency will impact the effectiveness of our interventions. We should start thinking of these different systems as either barriers or facilitators to educational opportunity for homeless children (Julianelle & Foscarinis, 2003). As children navigate the homeless experience, they confront multiple systems that influence, both positively and negatively, their ability to obtain educational opportunities. As we will see in the upcoming chapters, ameliorating the barriers or improving facilitators to both outcomes for children and youth and our practice is rooted in policy approaches and is a cornerstone of how schools address the problem of homelessness for their students.

Article Spotlight: Nooe and Patterson's 2010 article on an ecological perspective of homelessness is a very comprehensive look at many of the factors that can influence why people become and stay homeless. Nooe and Patterson (2010) present a model of homelessness that includes many different factors followed by text explaining each. It is a thorough introduction on the subject and is an excellent article to gain a lot of information on this topic quickly.

Nooe, R. & Patterson, D. (2010). The ecology of homelessness. *Journal of Human Behavior in the Social Environment, 20*, 105–152.

Using Evidence-Based Practice

As we practice with children experiencing homelessness, we should strive to use the evidence-based practice (EBP) model. Often when we think of EBP we only think of the science and research portion of it. While it is true that empirical evidence does play a role in EBP, it is only one of three aspects of the model. First and foremost, EBP is a process, a way to make practice decisions (Rubin & Babbie, 2010). We must include the clients and their attributes. We have to ask ourselves: What does the client bring and what are his or her wishes? For us practicing with homeless children, this means identifying and examining the different systems and factors inherent to an experience of homelessness in addition to the strengths of our clients. For example, we need to gain an understanding of the different barriers a homeless child faces. Next, we must leverage our practice experience and skills. In EBP, we have to use interventions that we as practitioners know how to use. For example, if behavior modification techniques have been shown to improve an outcome, but we have no experience with behavior modification techniques, we need to select a different intervention for our use. Finally, we need to examine what the available evidence tells us to be effective. Ideally this is the empirical research, but if there are little or no studies available, we can, at the very least, consult an expert.

The Role of School Social Workers and Other School-Based Practitioners

School social workers and other school-based practitioners play an important role in addressing the impact of experiencing homelessness on schools and students. In general, school social workers are often used to support the mission of a school and provide settings for both the faculty and staff to facilitate education and for students to learn (Massat, Constable, McDonald, & Flynn, 2009). Our school-based practice and efforts to help homeless children and youth often involves a lot of work and collaboration with not only other professionals in the school (e.g., teachers, administrators, lunch and transportation staff) but also other agencies and professionals outside of the school. We must remember that homelessness is not actually experienced *in* school. It is an issue outside of the purview of a school that impacts the facilitation of education, the purpose of a school. So when we address homelessness in our practice, we as school social workers or other school-based practitioners are tasked with ameliorating the negative impacts of experiencing homelessness, which occurs outside the school, on what happens inside the school, at the school-level as well as to individual students.

As a note, this book is part of a series on various populations or issues in school social work practice. While it is important to discuss homeless in a greater context, including strategies designed to return people to housing, this book focuses more on how we address homelessness in our school-based practice. Strategies to end homelessness and increase affordable housing are valuable discussions that deserve their own focus. We will discuss some background information on why people become homeless to build a foundation for our knowledge, but everything we will discuss will be in the context of how it impacts both the students and schools. As school-based practitioners, much of what we do while working with children and youth experiencing homelessness revolves around two things: first, we work to remove and address the barriers homeless children and youth face when pursuing education and then to do this, we typically administer and facilitate the provisions of the McKinney-Vento Homeless Assistance Act (MVA). The policy and its guidelines are why our practice, and thus our discussion about homeless children and youth, can afford to be a little idiosyncratic. Although there are many common factors between the homeless experiences and general poverty experiences, we are guided by a policy that specifically addresses homelessness and is a major foundation of our practice.

As we move through the rest of the book, we will use this chapter as a foundation. Homelessness is a complex experience that transcends simple explanations and interventions. On top of this, it is a growing concern for our schools and will continue to be an issue that communities must address. Ecological-systems perspective gives us a good way to organize our thinking on homelessness. This perspective will allow us to account for much of the complexity in an experience of homelessness, while still granting us a clear framework to develop our interventions.

Summary

Homelessness is often thought of as a status, meaning we like to think that one is either homeless or not homeless. However, this approach has confounded over 25 years of literature and does not allow for us to take into account all of the unique factors that are inherent to a homeless situation. Much of the complexity of homelessness stems from all of the different aspects and circumstances that impact outcomes. The federal definition of homelessness provides examples of how different situations, each with their own stressors and risk factors, can all be considered homeless. We should instead think of homelessness as an experience—it contains a multitude of different elements that can affect a given outcome. As we turn our thoughts into actions through our practice, the foundation underpinning our interventions should take into account the complexity of the systems that influence outcomes for homeless children by viewing them as either barriers or facilitators.

Finally, we must combine client attributes, practitioner knowledge and skills, and available evidence to be EBP practitioners. All three components of EBP must be included in our practice decisions. This book will be a guide to all three aspects of EBP with homeless children and youth. We will gain a better understanding of the clients we serve and find out a little more about the systems that can impact our practice. We will develop our knowledge and skills by examining the relevant policy that dominates our practice interventions as school social workers and other related professionals. Throughout this, we will be examining empirical studies and the literature to gives us a sturdy research-based foundation to practice with homeless children.

The rest of the book builds upon the foundation of this chapter. Now that we have a good base and understanding of our thinking about what homelessness is, we can move on to more detailed and nuanced information about homelessness in our practice. Chapter 2 will help us expand our foundation understanding of homelessness by looking at the literature of how homelessness impacts children and youth, develop an understanding of how the literature has shaped and been shaped by our thinking, and how people become homeless. We will then move on to a discussion of the MVA, the policy that guides our practice in both chapter 3, which includes a review of the policy, and chapter 4, which focuses more on the practice implications of the legislation. Using all of the information from the first four chapters, we will then discuss a practice perspective for our work with homeless children and youth in the final chapter.

Practice Takeaways

- Homelessness is a complex issue.
- Homeless is defined as those who lack a fixed, regular, and adequate nighttime residence.
- We should view homelessness as an experience, rather than a situation.
- There are many different situations that can still be considered homelessness.
- Ecological-systems theory provides a good way to organize the complexity of homelessness.

2

What We Know about Homelessness

Building a Foundation

"The path that leads to what we truly desire is long and difficult,
but only by following that path do we achieve our goal."

—*Master Splinter*

There is a lot of literature and information on homeless children, so much so that it is almost unmanageable. It makes it very difficult figuring out a good place to start for building our knowledge on children and youth experiencing homelessness. Much of the literature on children experiencing homelessness is descriptive in nature—it generally outlines the impact of homelessness on a given outcome, whether it is academic, health, behavior, or other. Organizing this chapter to provide meaningful information was a challenge. There is a lot of information and knowledge in general on the topic of child homelessness, but determining what is usable and actionable knowledge for school-based practitioners requires a frame of reference or context. In order to create a framework to examine the knowledge base on children and youth experiencing homelessness, we should review how evidence-based practice can help school social work practice in a little more detail.

School social work practice is very outcome oriented, meaning expected outcomes rather than a diagnosis or issue guides our practice (Massat, Constable, McDonald, & Flynn, 2009). Therefore we need to build our understanding around how experiencing homelessness for a school-aged child can impact our school-based outcomes. Typically, there are two types of evidence: the academic/empirical knowledge base and information based off of our experiences. This chapter is going to focus more on what the empirical knowledge base can tell us about the impact of experiencing homelessness on childhood outcomes. We can then help inform, shape, and put our experiences into an empirical context. The purpose of this chapter is to provide a general foundation and base to our knowledge on homelessness. The challenge in this is to keep an eye on how the information presented can help us determine the practice outcomes that guide our school social work practice.

To accomplish this, the chapter is structured in two parts. The first part gives us background information on homelessness and its impact on outcomes. This information is meant to be a good foundation for practitioners using evidence-based practice to develop a literature-informed understanding of the issue. The topics described and discussed will give us a solid understanding of the issue and how it has been addressed in the relevant research literature. The chapter starts with a brief introduction on the history of studies on homeless children and families. Next, the chapter provides a description of both the scope of homelessness and common demographics found in the literature. The discussion then switches to the reasons behind why families become homeless. Next the chapter provides findings on how homelessness children achieve academically, behave, and finally on their overall health. The next discussion is about clarifying how homelessness impacts these outcomes. The first half of the chapter concludes by building on the definition and conceptualization of child homelessness.

The second part of the chapter is about how homelessness impacts students and our schools. The chapter discusses the impact of residential instability on education. A brief review of why barriers and facilitators are important in the educational lives of homeless children and youth follows. The chapter discusses challenges to determining and using certain outcomes in our practice. Next is a discussion of the links between mental health, homelessness, and education. The chapter discusses long-term impacts of homelessness on children and youth, and then concludes with the school-wide impact of homelessness.

A Brief History on the Literature

One of the universals about practicing at a school is that invariably there is always someone who has worked there "forever." Oftentimes it is a secretary who has been there for 50 years, a teacher who has taught most of the other teachers' parents, or a principal who has overseen the school since before vinyl was popular. These people are often great resources for understanding the history and context of what happens at a school and why. Every now and then I will be supervising or talking with a social work student doing a field placement at a school and the conversation will turn to what happens at the school. The student usually says "in class, we discussed ..." or "we went over doing ... in this way, but the school does ..." There is usually a bit of concern from that student that what we learned in the most recent version of Allen-Meares or Bye and Alvarez is not necessarily matching up to what is being done at their school. After the student brings this up, I usually ask the student to go and talk to that one person who has the most experience or someone who can place what happens at the school into context. It is very important for us as practitioners to progress forward in our knowledge, skills, and experience, but still be mindful of the past. As we continue to develop our understanding of child homelessness and make sense of the literature, we must take a look at how our knowledge of homelessness and its impact on children and youth has developed and changed over time.

Child and family homelessness really became an issue in the literature around 1987. This is when some of the earliest studies on the topic were published, around the time the Stewart B. McKinney Act, later becoming the McKinney-Vento Act (MVA), was enacted. The first set of studies, dubbed "first generation" studies by Buckner in his 2008 systematic review, brought the severe mental health and health problems associated with homelessness to our consciousness. We have to remember that at this time, shelter systems and supports for people experiencing homelessness were typically designed to help single individuals without children. So when a family became homeless, they entered into a system that was unprepared to address their unique needs (Buckner, 2008). It brought attention for a need to form a deeper understanding of the issue when the findings from these early studies were published.

The "second-generation" of studies came about after 1991 according to Buckner (2008). This new generation of studies built upon the first set of publications by introducing rigor, with the help of funding, to better study the impact of homelessness. This set of studies aimed to clarify how homelessness impacts outcomes and three types of studies emerged in the last 25 years of literature on child homelessness. First, studies comparing homeless children to the general population gave us evidence that experiencing homelessness leads to poor outcomes. Next, several studies compared homeless children to their impoverished, but housed, peers without instruments that could allow for further comparisons to the general population. This is important because it allows us to determine whether homelessness children are "worse off" than poor children with housing, but it does not allow us to compare an overall impact of poverty. The final type of study addresses this limitation by using measures that allow for comparisons to the general population.

What Does the Literature Tell Us?

Again, most studies on homeless children and youth are descriptive in nature (Buckner, 2008). This provides findings that allow us to describe the impact of homelessness, but not necessarily determine what will help homeless children and youth. What we are able to say about this topic is really only outlining who experiences homelessness (the scope of the problem) and how it is impacting outcomes. This next section is going to provide a description of what we know by first discussing the scope of child homelessness and then discussing the impact of homelessness on academic, mental health, and physical health outcomes.

The Scope of Homelessness

Most estimates place the number of children and youth experiencing homelessness over the course of a year at approximately 3.2 million (National Coalition for the Homeless, 2009). These numbers are considered to be underestimations, as they only include those who are seeking services. So if a child is doubled-up (staying with friends or family in a nonpermanent basis) and does not seek or receive services, he or she would most likely not be included into a count of homelessness. Some estimates indicate that one out of every 50 children and youth experience homelessness (Anderson, 2011; National Center on Family Homelessness, 2009). Furthermore, in the estimations that the National Center on Family Homelessness (2009) uses, 75% of all homeless children are actually located within only a fifth of the states in the United States. Finally, homeless children and their families are considered to be the fastest growing segment of the homeless population (Dotson, 2011).

Typically, homeless families are headed by single females, up to 90% in some estimations (Dail, 1990, as cited in Anooshian, 2003). Studies have found that homeless single women with children tend to earn less than single males or females without children (Anooshian, 2003). Homeless mothers experience physical and sexual abuse at higher rates than other women (Bassuk et al., 1996). Furthermore, single homeless women and their children are separated at higher rates than their housed peers (Barrow & Laborde, 2008). In fact, homelessness is the major predictor of whether a child is taken from a parent (Cowal, Shinn, Weitzman, Stojanovic, & Labay, 2002; Culhane, Webb, Grim, Metraux, & Culhane, 2003). Homeless mothers are almost two times more likely to lose their children compared to their housed peers, even though many programs that serve homeless families are designed for family preservation (Barrow & Lawinski, 2009).

So what are the implications of this for our practice in schools? As we practice with children and youth experiencing homelessness, we must be highly cognizant of child welfare issues. Although we should always be aware of child welfare issues for all of our students in general, they take on a larger meaning and context for children and youth experiencing homelessness. As we will discuss in more detail later on in this chapter, experiencing homelessness may not cause problems, but they may exacerbate them, and as such, child welfare situations are an excellent example.

A common situation many female single-headed households find themselves in involves childcare and finding employment. These difficulties are compounded when experiencing homelessness. For example, the mother of a single-headed family residing in a shelter may be offered a job interview in a nearby establishment. The interview occurs during the day, and especially in summer her kids may have nowhere to go. So the mother is left with a dilemma: leave her kids unsupervised at the shelter and go to the interview, or skip the interview, which obviously ruins current employment chances but may negatively impact future ones as well. I have heard story after story of people who have run out to take the job interview and come back to find that social services has been called and their children are taken away. Now this can happen with housed single-headed households as well, but the public nature of experiencing homelessness or staying in a shelter is an added element in addition to the normal risk factors that can impact outcomes. This is not to say that homeless children and families always are going to be worse off, but it does highlight that we need to understand how homelessness can influence our outcomes.

We should also put our practice into a school and community context. We can conceptualize the school as a combination of the families, their issues, community agencies, and school faculty and staff (Massat, Constable, McDonald, & Flynn, 2009). Sometimes there are conflicting purposes between outside entities and the school. For example, child welfare agencies mainly focus on the safety of the child, whereas schools focus on education. In addition, shelters focus on providing refuge from the elements. Although the entities share some common goals, the purposes may differ, which will cause challenges. Our practice with children and youth experiencing homelessness will have us collaborate in an attempt to merge the differing purposes.

Impact of Experiencing Homelessness on Academics

Kids can be really fun to work with, especially when they smile. When a child genuinely smiles from happiness, it seems like every adult in the room smiles too. One of my favorite stories about working with homeless children happened when one of the great organizations I work with, Faces Without Places, decided to do a promotional video about their programming. They interviewed a handful of children they served about their experiences and their life. They asked one kid what he wanted to be when he grew up. He looked straight into the camera, and without hesitation, said with a big smile, "I want to be ice cream!"

Needless to say, all of the adults laughed, but what the child was really talking about is an interesting concept. His response was so wholesome, so childish, so just filled with happiness and hope that it just feels good to think about it. We forget that homeless children do not often get to have dreams such as this and from an early age have a sense of hopelessness about their future (Weinger, 1998). By being homeless, children often lose the ability to be children; to have dreams of what growing up could be that don't make sense to adults. This is important to us as school-based practitioners because many of our interventions are designed to eventually lead to positive outcomes for our clients as adults. We want to keep our students in school and graduate. We want to provide meaningful educational opportunities that turn into fulfilling lives for the children and youth we serve. So when we talk about academics and education, we are really talking about the future.

Article Spotlight: Hope is such an important aspect of resiliency. If you have hope, you can succeed. Many studies of hope are not conducted on poor urban youth, meaning our understanding of hope may not be congruent with how impoverished youth perceive their world. Dr. Dana Harley conducted a fantastic study on hope using Photovoice. She gave cameras to children and then conducting structured interviews to better understand how impoverished children perceive hope.

What she found was surprising. One child took a picture of a dilapidated gas station and called that hope. The child explained that even though the store had been robbed several times, it was still open. Another child took a picture of a tree and said that because it was still standing it was hopeful.

All of this indicates that our students experiencing homelessness and poverty may perceive the world in a very different way than we normally think. We should strive to find ways to empower students by giving them a voice. Dr. Harley's work does this and is definitely worth a read.

Harley, D. (In Press). Perceptions of hopelessness among low-income African American adolescents through the lens of Photovoice. *Journal of Ethnic & Cultural Diversity in Social Work.*

Harley, D. (2011). Perceptions of hope and hopelessness among low-income African American adolescents. (Electronic Thesis or Dissertation). Retrieved from https://etd.ohiolink.edu/

With the literature on the impact of homelessness on academic outcomes for homeless children and youth, truthfully we really only have "sound bites." We can say things like homeless children are seven times more likely to be truant than their peers (Nolan et al., 2013), but we often do not really translate it into action in practice. We must take every effort to turn our knowledge into practice as we serve children and youth experiencing homelessness (Walsh & Douglas, 2009). In general, homeless children and youth are at very high risk for missing an inordinate amount of school days (Miller, 2009a; Rafferty, Shinn, & Weitzman, 2004). On average, reading and math proficiency scores are 16% less than their peers (National Center on Family Homelessness, 2009). Dropout risk is elevated for children and youth experiencing homelessness (Jozefowicz-Simbeni & Israel, 2006). Some estimations of graduation rates indicate that less than 25% of homeless children make it through high school (National Center on Family Homelessness, 2009). For just about every academic outcome we can imagine, homeless children do poorly (Barwick & Siegel, 1996; Berliner, 2009; Buckner, 2008; Buckner, Bassuk, & Weinreb, 2001; Di Santo, 2012; Fantuzzo & Perlman, 2007; Fantuzzo, LeBoeuf, Brumley, & Perlman, 2013).

> Article Spotlight: A consistent source of information I regularly go to is the National Center for Family Homelessness' report on how each state ranks in terms of how they address homelessness. The report is a report card titled *America's Youngest Outcasts*, but I refer to it as the Report Card. It gives us a quick overview of how America is doing addressing homelessness, and provides lots of information on different outcomes. The coolest feature of the Report Card is that it provides rankings for each state and includes an overview of what the state is doing to help homeless children and youth. I always suggest practitioners briefly review their state to get a handle on what is going on in their backyard.

Impact of Experiencing Homelessness on Mental and Behavioral Health

Outside of facilitating the McKinney-Vento Act, we may often interact with homeless students through addressing mental health issues. The following is a common scenario that plays out in schools across the country. Phil was in third grade for the second time and got in a lot of trouble. Almost daily his teacher had to discipline him, and at least once a week he was sent to the office for acting out. Because of all the trouble he got into while in class, he was often isolated and separated from the other children. This made it very hard for him to make friends or build a social network. Then the other students somehow found out Phil stayed at the homeless shelter. They gave him a new name, "Philthy," which caused him to act out even worse than before, further isolating him. It got so bad that an interdisciplinary team was put together to help Phil.

Children and youth experiencing homelessness suffer from a multitude of mental health issues (Chambers et al., 2013; Hodgson, Shelton, van den Bree,

---

& Los, 2013). These children have higher rates of anxiety and depression (Menke, 1998), among other issues. The isolation that many of these children experience prevents normal and healthy relationship building and maintaining (Menke, 2000). Children experiencing homelessness may be predisposed to mental health issues as these problems are often cited as a reason for why families become homeless (Nooe & Patterson, 2010).

Even though homeless children suffer from elevated rates of mental and behavioral health issues, I want to caution and remind us to examine other systems that may be at play. When the school psychologist was giving a psychometric test to Phil, she noticed that he was squinting really hard to read instructions. The nurse was notified and it turned out that Phil had a vision problem. The school social worker was able to connect Phil and his mother to a resource that provided him glasses. The school moved him to a different class wherein he had a fresh start and he then became a model student. Apparently, the vision problems had frustrated him so much that he acted out, his continual acting out in class labeled him as a problem student, and a vicious cycle was created. His academic situation, compounded with the other stressors in his life, led to poor academic performance and what people thought were severe mental health problems (he was not oppositional or defiant, just nearsighted).

Impact of Experiencing Homelessness on Health

Children and youth experiencing homelessness often suffer from a host of health maladies. These children suffer from asthma at higher rates than other children (Cutuli, Herbers, Rinaldi, Masten, & Oberg, 2010; Grant et al., 2007), often thought to be caused by poor shelter conditions homeless families often find themselves in. Oftentimes we group homeless children and youth in with other at-risk youth (Panter-Brick, 2004), but this can belie the complexity of the issue. Along these lines, many homeless children may not have the same developmental opportunities as other, housed youth. Cramped emergency shelter conditions or dangerous debris located in abandoned or condemned buildings do not allow for younger children to explore their environment. Physical growth is impacted, especially in terms of height (Fiereman et al., 1991). In addition, homeless children and youth are often in the lower percentiles of weight-height measurements (Fiereman et al., 1991). Hunger is also a major problem for homeless children, though somewhat paradoxically, obesity is also a problem for homeless children and youth (Richards & Smith, 2007). Many times school lunch is the only meal a homeless child may have over the course of a day.

Poor access to healthcare can be a severe barrier for the homeless in general (Gewirtz, Hart-Shegos, & Medhanie, 2008), and can impact the healthy development of children and youth. Other aspects of healthcare can be barriers to being healthy. For example, medication literacy can be difficult and homeless parents may have trouble providing the correct medicine or doses to their children (Sleath et al., 2006). Homeless children have elevated risks for substance abuse issues (Salomonsen-Sautel et al., 2008). Some estimates place lifetime use for children and youth who have experienced homelessness from 66% to 90% (Salomonsen-Sautel et al., 2008). In addition, homeless children and youth are at greater risk for contracting HIV/AIDS than their peers (Rotheram-Borus, Koopman, & Ehrhardt, 1991).

Homelessness is not a normal experience, and we see this across academic, mental health/behavioral, and health outcomes. In almost every situation, those experiencing homelessness are often at either a disadvantage or high risk for poor performance. Now we need to understand why this is so. The literature on homelessness does provide some clues to help us understand and clarify how homelessness impacts children and youth.

Can We Clarify How Homelessness Impacts Children and Youth?

Is There a Continuum of Poverty?

Earlier, we went over how homelessness is bad for children to experience. Again, homeless children and youth have higher proportions of health problems, awful academic achievement, and massively high mental health problems (Barwick & Siegel, 1996; Berliner, 2009; Buckner, 2008; Buckner, Bassuk, & Weinreb, 2001; Chambers et al., 2013; Di Santo, 2012; Fantuzzo & Perlman, 2007; Fantuzzo, LeBoeuf, Brumley, & Perlman, 2013; Fierman et al., 1991; Hodgson, Shelton, van den Bree, & Los, 2013;). Study after study corroborates this in their findings, but how come? This is where understanding the history of research on child homelessness comes in handy. That first generation of studies found that experiencing homelessness had detrimental impacts to development (Buckner, 2008). The question soon turned to why? Out of this questioning came a conceptual approach to homelessness for children. Conceptually, many studies are based on the thinking that homelessness is the lowest point of a continuum of poverty (Buckner, 2008). Homeless children perform worse on outcomes, followed by impoverished but housed kids, and finally housed and not impoverished children would generally score best on a given measure. Here is the logic for this approach: All children have risk factors that can contribute to a given outcome, impoverished children have additional factors that put them at higher risk for poor results, and homelessness has a further set of elements on top of those that lead to troublesome ends. This theoretically means that homeless children should be "worse-off" than impoverished housed children, who should then be "worse-off" than children who do not experience poverty. But does this continuum hold up empirically?

Many studies address this by conducting studies that compare homeless children to their impoverished, but housed peers (Buckner, 2008; Buckner et al., 2001). Comparing youth experiencing homelessness to children who are housed, but in poverty, allows for comparisons that facilitate a better understanding of whether experiencing homelessness leads to poorer outcomes than just being poor. Finding that homeless children continuously perform worse would confirm a theoretical continuum of poverty. In an excellent systematic review on the literature of homeless children, Buckner (2008) examined the knowledge base to see if a continuum of poverty emerged. He found that in over 25 years of empirical literature, a consistent continuum of poverty did not materialize. There were too many inconsistencies across the 25 years of literature to clearly state that homeless children were persistently worse off. Several studies actually found that homeless children performed better than their peers.

Similar to how a school social work intern should better understand the context of a school, we should examine Buckner's 2008 review in the context of the history of research on the topic. Once we established that children who experience homelessness are suffering from poor outcomes, we needed to understand the extent: Contrasted to similar comparison groups, how much of an impact does homelessness have on a child? Did our theoretical understanding of homelessness hold up? This valuable systematic review did not necessarily provide solid evidence that our understanding of a continuum is correct. So now we need to figure out why. Buckner (2008) commented on several possible reasons. First, he discusses methodological (research-based) reasons. Examples of methodological issues across studies were that not all studies used the same groups or types of groups, measures were not consistent, and other studies had problems with internal inconsistency, meaning that in a given study, younger children could have been impacted more than older children experiencing homelessness. Despite the research-based methodological challenges, these are still relatively weak reasons for the overall inconsistency in 25 years of literature.

Article Spotlight: I cite Buckner's 2008 systematic review often in this section. I rely on this article a lot, but I do this because it is an excellent source for understanding the history of research on homeless children and youth. This well-done review covers almost the entirety of articles published since roughly 1987. When I am asked for a good article to introduce someone to the topic, I always suggest this article. It is an excellent summary of very important and salient research on children and youth experiencing homelessness. I strongly suggest that anyone who is interested in the topic should give it a read. It is a comprehensive review of all the published articles on comparisons between homeless children and their impoverished but housed peers. It gives a quick but comprehensive review of the thinking behind much of what is discussed in this section.

Buckner, J. (2008). Understanding the impact of homelessness on children: Challenges and future research directions. *American Behavioral Scientist, 51*, 721–736.

Historical and Political Reasons

First, child homelessness was not always considered to be an issue for practitioners, policy-makers, and other stakeholders. As we saw when we went over the history of studies on children and youth experiencing homelessness, this issue is a relatively new one for researchers and practitioners. Because of this, we did not, and some will argue still do not, know the best methodologies of understanding the impact of homelessness. Furthermore, although the MVA gives us a definition of homelessness that is closest to relative universal acceptance, only in 2002 were all states accepting MVA funds following the same definition. Previously it was up to the states to determine who was eligible for services. These factors all play a role in the inconsistencies in the literature.

Ecological-Systems Perspective

One of the suggested reasons for inconsistencies in findings on the comparisons between homeless and housed impoverished youth is rooted in our ecological-systems perspective. We need to examine differences in the environment and systems of various homeless situations. These differences may be the cause of the inconsistency we have found on the topic. For example, a family who lives out of their car will have different systems in play than a family who lives in a transitional housing program. Treating studies that use a sample of children living out of cars to ones examining children living in a transitional housing program as similar studies confounds our understanding of the issue. And as we have seen in over 25 years of the literature, this prevents us from making conclusive statements on findings.

So where do we go from here? An area on the literature of homelessness focuses on typologizing the experience (Culhane, Metraux, Park, Schretzman, & Valente, 2007; Danesco & Holden, 1998; Huntington, Buckner, & Bassuk, 2008; Kuhn & Culhane, 1998). This means researchers have been trying to determine if there are different "types" of homeless experiences. Like we discussed in chapter 1, treating all homeless situations as the same (i.e., a status) can be problematic. For example, a family who has been living in and out of shelters for years is very different than a normally stable family who lost their housing due to a natural disaster. That is why many feel it is important to identify different types of homelessness: In order to truly address the needs of our clients, we need to understand the systems at work in each experience of homelessness.

What Others Have Done to Typologize Homelessness

Oftentimes researchers try to typologize by time or shelter utilization (Kuhn & Culhane, 1998). This has led to our understanding homelessness as chronic, episodic, or temporary. Others try to typologize by the level of functioning (Huntington, Buckner, & Bassuk, 2008). A good example of this would be to take an outcome or outcomes and find categories of students statistically. So we may find that homeless children and youth fall into patterns of school attendance or test scores. Many studies usually focus their efforts on typologizing homeless individuals, but families also follow similar patterns (Culhane et al., 2007). These studies indicate that homelessness is not the same for everyone. By finding that there are different types of homelessness, our understanding of homelessness as an experience is bolstered.

Ways We Can Typologize as Practitioners

The ways we discussed for typologizing those experiencing homelessness can be difficult for us to do in our school-based practice. It is important for us to have a background, but we need to figure out a way to examine the different types of homelessness that may be present in our service areas. I think a good place to start is for us to look at the options a family has when they become homeless. These different options could all be considered homeless, but bring their own barriers or facilitators that will impact our practice.

Options Facing Homeless Families

When I teach a course on homelessness and poverty, I really try to think of ways I can attempt to give students the opportunity to see things from a homeless family's perspective. One way I have done this that most students find interesting is to go over the different types of housing options that a family has when they lose their housing. As I plan this lecture, I always think of Cadillac Escalades, or really, creative unorthodox decision-making homeless parents use to provide for their children. This story is about the options homeless families face when they lose housing.

Vignette: Cadillac Escalades

Like schools, the staff parking lot at a homeless shelter is usually filled with modest and prudent automobiles. Salaries usually do not allow for flashy and gaudy cars that make heads turn. Clients at this particular transitional housing facility were allowed to park their cars, if they had one, with the staff cars so the lot was usually filled with simple sedans, reasonable rides, and worn-out "whips." However, one Wednesday morning two parking spots were occupied by the auto of the newest family to join the program. Looming over the lot sat a bright white, relatively new, Cadillac Escalade. The gaudy and ostentatious sport utility vehicle (SUV) did not look right next to the fleet of cars the clients and staff drove. At this point in time, Escalades were the choice of celebrities to show off and were enormous luxury vehicles. Most people at the shelter thought the car belonged to someone visiting, but when the SUV was still there on Thursday, people began to ask around to find out to whom it belonged. Very quickly everyone knew that it belonged to the new family.

Once people found out the SUV belonged to a client, suspicions grew and jealous anger crept into the clients quickly, and to staff members shortly after.

People could not understand how a person could afford an Escalade and be homeless. Most people just thought the family was "stupid" and not in need of any help. If they sold the Escalade, people reasoned, then they would not have to worry about being homeless.

I was just as suspicious and more than a little jealous, but I thought I would ask anyway why this family had a Cadillac Escalade. The father of the family explained to me that he leased the Escalade two years ago when things were better. He told me that both he and his wife were working then and rather than saving money for a rainy day, they decided to spend the extra cash on a treat for themselves. Then they both lost their jobs, but not their lease. They were able to prop up their situation with small part-time jobs and jaunts into day labor, but they conceded that they would eventually be losing their home. The father explained to me that when he and his wife looked at their finances, they realized that they could not afford both rent and the car, but could continue to make payments on the car with their sporadic income. This was important he reasoned, because an Escalade was big enough for two small kids to sleep in the back and the parents to sleep in the front two seats. With a bed sheet partition hanging in the center of the SUV, it was almost as if the girls had their own room. Plus, he told me that while the kids were in school he and his wife could still get to work or search for a job.

He really wanted to get rid of the lease, but the SUV served a purpose. It did cause problems; some agencies were hesitant about serving the family who lived in a conspicuous luxury vehicle and he told me that his motivations were questioned often. However, after hearing his story my jealousy turned to admiration. Like many precariously housed families, they had a tough decision to make about how to best provide for their children. At this point in telling the story, most of my class goes from wondering why a homeless family would have a luxury SUV to nodding in understanding and admiration for finding an innovative way to survive.

Our understanding of the history of literature on child homelessness allows us to see that our knowledge is only starting to focus on gaining a deeper understanding of the issue. And one of those ways researchers have focused on is to determine categories that differentiate the experience of homelessness for children and youth. Not many homeless families are going to have the option of using a luxury SUV as a defacto recreation vehicle, but making tough decisions about where to go when housing is lost is common. Although there may be a myriad of actual housing options, we can focus on roughly six categories. This will also allow us to clarify some definitions that are often thrown about when we discuss homelessness.

First, families can end up in public places such as a park or "skid-row" type of area. As we think of a continuum, this should be at the farthest end. These are experiences that have the least amount of support and can sometimes be illegal. Many cities have public squares or parks that are known to be where the homeless congregate. We should think of these spaces as areas that lack any sort of structure to provide shelter. The next category on our continuum would be structures not fit for human habitation. These include luxury SUVs, garages, attics, sheds, and the like. They provide a little more shelter from the elements, but no other supports. Next, families may find temporary shelter through either motels or emergency shelters. Neither are long-term solutions, nor do they provide any services to find housing. Emergency shelters may not necessarily be for emergencies such as a natural disaster. This reflects our traditional thinking of homelessness for families as being a temporary time period families need to recover from. We should instead follow how HUD defines an emergency shelter: a temporary facility that provides overnight shelter (24 CFR 91.5 [Title 24 Housing and Urban Development; Subtitle A Office of the Secretary, Department of Housing and Urban Development; Part 91 Consolidated Submissions for Community Planning and Development Programs; Subpart A General]). Next, doubling-up falls on this continuum. Oftentimes this involves moving in with friends or relatives, meaning there is some relationship available. Although people have moved in temporarily with family and friends over the years, it is a relatively new experience added to the definition of homelessness. Finally, transitional housing facilities would be at the farthest end on a continuum of homeless options. These are facilities that provide overnight shelter in addition to support services.

These are six rough, overarching categories of where families end up when homeless. It is not meant to be an exhaustive list, nor is the continuum provided set in stone. What this list provides is a way for us to organize the situations and options the homeless families we practice with face. From our discussion on the MVA, we understand that we will be required to collaborate with outside agencies to help homeless children in our schools. This understanding, coupled with our knowledge of ecological-systems perspectives means we need to examine all of the systems within each option.

How Do People Become Homeless?

The etiology of homelessness is the official academic term for our understanding of why people become homeless and then stay homeless. An important aspect of addressing any issue is to determine how people come to have a problem, and what prevents improvement in the situation. Nooe and Patterson (2010) advocate for use of the ecological-systems perspective to help explain the causes of homelessness. Typical arguments about the reasons people or families become homeless revolve around two ideas. Either families become homeless because of individual factors or systems, or structural systems are in place that lead to homelessness situations. Viewing homelessness as either a cause of individual *or* structural reasons is overly reductionistic. For example, imagine if we could give every homeless person a million dollars. For some, this would end their homeless experience permanently. For others however, this would not address perhaps the mental health reasons a person became homeless. Similarly, if we were to take any city in America and build two skyscrapers the size of the Empire State Building filled with housing units and only charged $20 a month to live there, would this solve homelessness in the city? Sure, some people just need the affordable housing, but others have different reasons why they became homeless. Both of these examples highlight why we need to examine homelessness as a combination of both individual and structural factors. An ecological-systems perspective will help us organize and understand the etiology of homelessness. The following sections will discuss individual systems, structural systems, and how they interact. Each of the systems that we will go over was identified in Nooe and Patterson's (2010) fantastic model of homelessness using the ecological-systems perspective.

Individual Systems

This section will discuss several common individual systems that can impact whether a person or family becomes homeless. Some of these factors can be addressed in our school-based practice, but unfortunately, some will not. Even though we may not be able to address some systems directly in practice, it is still important to understand what factors are at play for our clients. Some factors, family violence for example, have been discussed earlier and will not appear here.

Social Support

Homelessness is an isolating experience (Anooshian, 2005) in and of itself. Empirically, several studies have found that homeless families have smaller

---

circles of support than other families (Bassuk et al., 1996). In pure numbers, some studies have found that homeless mothers have fewer members in their social network (Bassuk et al., 1997). They meet with other family members less often and generally do not feel that they have others to count on (Duval & Vincent, 2009). This means that the support a typical family may have in raising children may be absent or unavailable for homeless families. For example, some families may be able to coordinate carpools or transportation plans to get their kids to school. This option may not be available to a family living in a shelter.

Maltreatment

Negative childhood experiences can often lead to problems in adulthood. Homelessness can often be characterized as a violent experience (Anooshian, 2005; Chambers et al., 2013) and different forms of abuse and neglect are common. For teens especially, abuse and victimization are major risk factors for homelessness (Tyler, Whibeck, Hoyt, & Cauce, 2004). Sexual abuse is consistently found to be a major reason why many children run away from home (Johnson, Rew, & Sternglanz, 2006), but it is an experience that children in homeless families still face. Experiencing abuse or neglect may interrupt developmental processes for children and youth (Nooe & Patterson, 2010), which may make it harder for these children to develop meaningful relationships later in life (Anooshian, 2005).

Health Status

Earlier in this chapter we discussed the impact that experiencing homelessness has on health for children and youth. Here we will discuss how health status can lead to homelessness. Chronic health problems are common to those experiencing homelessness (Nooe & Patterson, 2010). Disabilities and chronic medical conditions can lead to bankruptcy and job loss (Himmelstein, Warren, & Woolhandler, 2005). If we think about a family who is already struggling to afford daily expenses and housing, adding a medical problem that requires long-term or expensive short-term costs can be extremely detrimental.

Substance Abuse

Substance abuse issues are oft-cited as a major factor in why some individuals and families become homeless. Several studies have found that those experiencing homelessness tend to have higher rates of addiction and substance abuse problems than the general population (Nyamathi, Hudson,

Greengold, & Leake, 2012; Salomonsen-Sautel, 2008)). However we must use caution in saying that substance use and abuse *cause* people to become homeless. There are many other factors that can be coupled with substance abuse that can lead to experiencing homelessness. For example, dual diagnosis is often common in homeless folks with substance abuse disorders (Nooe & Patterson) and it is difficult to tease out whether a mental health diagnosis leads to substance abuse and vice versa, much less determine whether one or the other caused homelessness. Another factor that can harm people experiencing homelessness form obtaining housing is that often shelters or housing programs have rules about sobriety. Anecdotally, I have seen many people unable to get the housing help they need because of substance abuse issues. Rather than being offered treatment help or designing housing programs to offer help with sobriety, many are turned back to the streets and emergency shelters.

Structural Systems

Structural systems can be a major factor as to why families become homeless. These are often society or macro level factors that impact what happens at a micro level. The next couple of paragraphs are descriptions of common structural systems our clients and their families often face. By no means is it meant to be an exhaustive list.

Employment

The first direct experience that I remember with someone experiencing homelessness (outside of panhandlers) felt odd. I was in eighth grade and my youth group was volunteering at a homeless shelter. We were helping to serve dinner and provide entertainment (we had a couple musical numbers prepared). One of the first ladies to whom I served barbecue chicken had served me fried chicken at a fast food restaurant about an hour earlier. She was still in her work uniform as she came through the line, and it was awkward for both of us. It was odd for me because I never thought people with jobs could be homeless. We often think that homeless people are unemployed, but that often is not the case (US Conference of Mayors, 2005). Many of those experiencing homelessness are employed, but just not at a sufficient wage. In addition, many of the jobs do not offer benefits that can act as a buffer in the event of a medical crisis. Furthermore, homeless individuals may not be able to provide documentation needed to begin employment. Also, the longer one experiences homelessness, the less chance one has of obtaining a job; long-term lack of employment can lead to a decrease in skills and other work related tasks and attitudes (Nooe & Patterson, 2010). These subsystems to employment (wage, skills, knowledge, etc.) are major factors to why people become and stay homeless.

Housing Costs and Availability

One of the most common reasons attributed to why people become and stay homeless is the lack of affordable housing. In the last 40 years, millions of low-rent units were lost due to various reasons (Daskal, 1998). In particular, the loss of single room occupancy units has dramatically increased the odds of many experiencing homeless. As cities gentrify, affordable housing is often a casualty. This creates a competition for remaining units, which leads to a rise in rent. Those with individual issues (addictions, mental health issues, etc.) that may prevent them from competing for available housing often become homeless.

Healthcare Costs

A good example of how individual and structural systems are interrelated is through healthcare. As we discussed earlier, people experiencing homelessness often have chronic health problems that lead to homelessness. This stressor is often compounded by the cost of treatment. Individuals and families must make decisions about what costs will be paid, and often this conundrum leads to homelessness. Estimates before the Affordable Healthcare Act enactment placed more than a third of homeless people with no health insurance, period (Nooe & Patterson, 2010). The impact of the Affordable Healthcare Act has yet to be seen, though the availability of insurance theoretically should help.

How Individual and Structural Systems Intertwine

The following is a good example of how individual and structural factors can converge to impact a situation. It is set in a rural town and is about a family who faces some tough decisions and situations. The vignette itself switches from the perspective of the social worker to the perspective of the family and back throughout the story.

Vignette: Elmer and Layla

I first met Elmer and Layla when they became residents at the transitional housing program and facility in my city. I learned the two had been from the surrounding rural area during the intake assessment. They used to live about 70 miles from the shelter in a small two-bedroom house on half an acre of land two miles from the main road in their town. Elmer's grandfather had built the house sometime in the 1920s or 1930s and passed it down to Elmer's father and then to Elmer. I learned Layla was Elmer's 10-year old only child from his marriage to Theresa. The two had Layla relatively late in life and by the time he entered the shelter he was nearing 50.

After the intake, I helped to set up some treatment goals for the family. Layla had not been in school for a month or two so the first thing done was to contact the school and the school social worker. The next day she was enrolled and in a class before lunch. The school social worker contacted her previous school and found out that she had some severe behavioral issues. So in conjunction with the school social worker, I was able to refer her to some services to address the problems and get her into a counseling program done through an agency contracting with the school. Layla's treatment goals were relatively easy to address and once she received some counseling, she became a model student and excelled in school. I had a much more difficult time with Elmer.

* * *

Elmer was not the type of smart that graded well in school but he was the first in his family to pass twelfth grade and graduate. He mostly worked for the local mechanics in the small rural area where he lived, but work began to dwindle as his neighbors in town could no longer afford to get their cars fixed. His last job before he came to the shelter was with the only gas station/oil change place on the main road in his town. He worked there for about five years until the gas station closed down about the time his wife was diagnosed with cancer.

Theresa and Elmer's first date was senior prom and from that night they were inseparable. Two weeks after Elmer's graduation they were married and the two immediately tried to have kids, but for years they had no luck. Eventually, the two had given up and made peace that "it was not meant to be." But that was until they had a surprise in their late thirties—Layla was born. She was loved by both Elmer and Theresa for years before she was actually born, so when she finally arrived it was into a world of warmth. Both did their best to "raise her right"—Theresa took care of most of the day-to-day activities while Elmer did his best to keep food on the table and the lights on.

Elmer was the type of dad who was very good at adding posts to an old twin bed frame to make a canopy bed for his "little princess" or repainting and repurposing shelves to coordinate with the pink sheets that Theresa and Layla picked out on one of the rare trips to the Sears in the city. Homework, school, and the emotional care were left to Theresa. Elmer considered himself to be from an era where men "just don't show" emotions or too much affection. So when Theresa died, Elmer had no clue what to do for himself or Layla.

* * *

The first several times I spoke with Elmer he always sounded like a proselytizing grandfather. "I ain't never taken nothin' I didn' earn. I don' need no handouts," was a common saying he told to me over and over again. In fact, he always smoked his cigarettes by himself on the opposite porch from all of the other residents because he "ain't one of them." It was these beliefs he espoused that prevented him from signing up for Medicaid or other assistance he was eligible for before and during things going bad.

* * *

Living in a deep rural area their entire lives meant Elmer and Theresa were adept at combining trips to maximize the almost 150 mile roundtrip it would take to get to and from the city. The first time Theresa complained of fatigue and back pain was two days before one of their trips. They would often plan for a month or two to combine a trip to the shopping mall, Super PartitionMart, the pool, and the movies into one very long day. Elmer wanted her to go to see the doctor for the pain but Theresa reasoned that there would be no time in their next trip without cutting something out and they promised Layla they would take her to see the newest princess animated film. She wrote "go to doc" on the to-do list of their next trip, which was tentatively scheduled for another month or two out.

Theresa's physical health deteriorated over those two months. She could no longer play tag with Layla and struggled to keep up with her when they would walk to the local Dollar General. When Layla had her school picture taken with a "Kool-Aid moustache," Theresa knew she had to see someone for the pain—that was a detail she would never have let slip, but she wanted to wait until the scheduled trip. The money and time it took to get to the city was too much, she reasoned. She was in more and more pain, so two weeks before their scheduled visit to the city Elmer did something he rarely did: he "overruled" his wife. He so much hated watching his wife writhe viciously from pain that he made an appointment on her behalf and the three of them got in his truck and went to the city.

When I finally developed enough of a rapport and trust with Elmer for him to tell me his story in detail, he described the first hospital trip like a horror movie, "you know in one them scary movies, when the person does something they don' think will kill 'em, but we all know they ain't makin' it out, that's what it is like to write "none" on the insurance line when I come to think of it."

When I asked about Medicaid, the proselytizing started, "Medicaid is for people that ain't wanna work so I ain't want it. My job didn't offer none (health insurance) but it ain't never been a big deal before," he said, "we always paid our taxes and been good people."

* * *

Theresa had cancer that had already started to spread. The doctor suggested some sort of aggressive treatment and both were on board. Even though the gas station had closed down, Elmer always found a way to get the gas money so Theresa could receive treatments in the city. She did her best to make sure Layla went to school and did her homework. Layla did her best to be like Ramona Quimby in her books. She, like Ramona, knew something was going on in the family, but knew it was her role to not say a word. For a little while, things went back to normal.

On a funereal overcast morning, the doctor solemnly eulogized the treatment results: they did not work. He offered suggestions for other treatments that could buy some time, but he always said the prognosis was dim. At best, new treatments could prolong her life. While listening to Layla read about Ramona Quimby to Elmer, Theresa whispered to the doctor and then made eye contact with Elmer, "I want as much of this as I can." The new treatments began shortly thereafter.

"I ain't never made that much in one paycheck," Elmer whispered about the first bill he received as he was hiding it from Theresa. It was the first bill in Elmer's life that he did not pay on time. At the hospital, when asked how we would be paying for the treatment he always said bill me later and they remembered. Theresa did not find the bills until the envelopes were too much to hide. By this time she was confined mostly to the bed and only short trips to the bathroom. Her skin was a pale colorless yellow and it was often a fight for her to stay awake. It took particular amounts of strength and focus for anything else.

She was always very resourceful and within days, despite the fatigue, came up with a solution, "Elmer, we got to have a grown-up talk."

"It's OK baby, when you need to go, go," accepting it was time to say goodbye.

"It ain't about that. I found the bills—shh, don't say nothing til you hear me out. I want you to divorce me—don't make that face. This ain't about love baby. I know you love me and Layla, but I talked with a lawyer . . ."

"You shouldn't be wastin' your energy . . ."

"We can write up a divorce paper that says the debt goes with me. Ed—shh, you know he is a good man, Ed says he'll be our lawyer for free. He done this before," she told him as she pulled out the papers she already had drawn up, "Ed knows the judge here, you know him too, Everett; both said it'll be a favor for us cause you always been good and honest with they cars all them years."

"I ain't doin' it!" It was the first time he had ever raised his voice to Theresa. "I ain't lettin' you die alone." And that was the end of the conversation. A couple weeks later, about 20 minutes after Layla finished reading the last chapter of *Ramona Quimby Age 8* to Theresa, she passed away. Several days after that, Theresa was laid to rest in the same cemetery the town had used for at least four generations.

* * *

"Debt collection is like a semi," he confided in me in one of our sessions, "it takes a while to start up but then when it gets to highway speed it don' stop."

I was not sure if the debt collection agency took his house or if he had to sell it or what the situation really was; he would only explain it one way: he "lost the house."

* * *

Elmer and Layla's lives skidded into oncoming traffic soon after losing the house. Elmer was never good at dealing with emotions, so those of a grieving 10-year old were especially difficult. Layla soon "went crazy" as he put it. At school the teachers and staff cared for her situation but their patience grew thin eventually, leading to a suspension. On top of this, they had been staying with an elderly friend who had even less patience for Layla's "issues." And once Layla had to stay at home all day, the friend could not take it anymore so she politely, but very firmly, asked the two to leave.

For the next month or so the two bounced from place to place. Because Elmer and Layla were only staying in places long enough to burn through the good will Elmer had built up over the years, the school bus did not know where to pick her up, so Layla only went to school when the two were staying within walking distance. Not wanting himself or Layla to become more of a pariah in town coupled with limited job prospects, he loaded up his truck and headed to the city. He had enough money saved up from day labor to stay for two weeks in a weekly motel, which he figured would be enough time to find some employment. From there he could get a place to live and then he would get Layla into school. He did not want to enroll her in school and then pull her out in case the place he found was in a different district.

Fifteen days since he and Layla moved into the city he still had no job prospects. The only option he thought of was to sleep in the truck. He found a quiet, well-lit spot near the main road and parked there for the night. At two in the morning both Layla and Elmer were woken up by a gentle knocking on the window. It was a police officer who noticed the truck. The cop asked them what they were doing there and asked to see identification for both Elmer and Layla. Elmer could hear dispatch confirm that she was not listed as a missing or exploited child and confirmed that he was her father. The cop came back to the car and told them to move along. Before he left, he gave them the card of a case manager at the local homeless coalition and said they could help. After five more nights and two more brushes with the cops, he finally swallowed his pride and drove to the place on the card and was admitted into the transitional housing program.

*　*　*

Elmer finally relented and let people help him. Once he made this breakthrough, things changed very quickly for him and Layla. He got into a program that furthered his mechanic training and allowed me to contact some people in my professional network on his behalf. This led to a sustainable position in the City Garage working maintenance on the municipal fleet. Layla continued to flourish in school and made a lot of friends. On their last day in the shelter I saw Layla reading *Ramona Quimby, Age 8* to her dad. She stopped and said, "Momma always loved the ending—they finish up a happy family."

What We Learned

This story provides a couple of clear examples in which different systems at both micro and macro levels intersect. Up to this point our discussion about homelessness and the various systems that impact the situation has focused mainly outside of the school. Here is where we start moving the discussion from what happens outside of the school to how we as school social workers and other related professionals address homelessness in our school-based practice. Rather than just focus solely on identifying an issue and discussing it as we did earlier, we will start to put different factors into a school-based practice context.

Earlier we discussed how homelessness is an experience with many different unique systems or factors inherent to each situation. Locale-specific factors are an excellent example of macro-level systems that can impact outcomes. Because homelessness is mainly thought to be an urban issue, service areas in suburban and rural locales may not have access to the same services. In the story, Elmer's family lived a great distance from the city and thus the services available. Trips to the hospital had to be planned out weeks in advance, and the cost of transportation had to be budgeted. This is similar to what many school social workers and other related professionals face when practicing with children and youth experiencing homelessness. In cities in which public transportation is readily available and relatively reliable, transporting students between schools is easier than in rural locales with no public transportation.

Thinking more about location-specific factors, we need to be aware of the resources available in our service area. Elmer's family was very familiar with the people living in the town—from knowing the judge, the lawyer, and people to stay with. I bring this up because as we identify children and youth experiencing homelessness for services, we must be acutely aware of typical avenues homeless children and families take to find shelter. If we are in a rural area like the one Elmer and Layla reside in, we would need to utilize both the interpersonal networks available (as far as our ethics allow) in addition to the formal services available. For example, at the end of the story the school social worker was in regular contact with the case manager at the transitional housing facility, so helping a new child at the shelter such as Layla get into school was a normal process. Both formal and informal systems in a locale can be a big factor in identifying and intervening with homeless school-age children.

This story gives an example of how individual factors, such as beliefs about public services, intersect with systemic factors (e.g., availability of insurance, employment). Elmer waited a while before he sought or received services, which not only led him to experience homelessness, but as a result, hindered Layla's academic achievement. When working in our school-based practice, we may find ourselves working to reduce shame felt by homeless children and families and eliminating stigma in our service area. Many homeless families do not want to be identified for services, so we must create environments in which children and families feel comfortable disclosing their situation. Along these lines we should prepare our service areas for the needs of homeless children and youth (Canfield et al., 2012). We need to work to ensure that the environment of the school must be accepting and conducive to helping homeless families.

This story was included to be a point at which we can move from talking about homeless in a general way to speaking more about how school social workers and other related professionals address homelessness as an issue. So where do we start? We can use our ecological-systems perspective to help us frame how we can help in a situation such as the one described. First and foremost we need to remember that changing one system will then impact other systems. These can be big changes, such as Elmer "losing" the house impacting Layla's academic experience, to smaller more subtle changes, such as when Theresa was in too much pain to notice that Layla went to school with a Kool-Aid mustache. Everything we do in our school-based practice with homeless children and youth will have a knock-on effect. Identifying a child for services will impact transportation systems, enrollment systems, and almost any other school-related system.

We must also remember that the whole is larger than the sum of its parts, according to an ecological-systems perspective. When we address homelessness we cannot just focus solely on one aspect or system in a homeless child's life. Obviously some issues may be more pressing than others, but we cannot forget that we should eventually address multiple systems. For Layla, only addressing the academic systems would not have addressed her grief issues. Only by addressing both could Layla flourish. Our school-based practice with homeless children and youth should take a similar approach by addressing multiple systems when possible.

Summary

This chapter was designed to give us a good foundation on what the literature says about child and youth homelessness, because we need to develop a good base of knowledge about our topic to better understand and facilitate our practice with this population. Earlier in the chapter we reviewed the history of studies on homeless children and youth in order to understand how we have come to our current understanding and focus of the issue. After this we looked at the scope of the issue and looked at why people became homeless. We went over the general impact of homelessness on academic, behavioral and mental health, and physical health. We tried to come to a theoretical understanding of homelessness in comparison to those housed but still experiencing homelessness. Our examination of the literature led us to question whether we could determine types of homeless experiences. This was followed by an overview of what it is like to experience homelessness.

Now that we have a solid understanding on the impact of homelessness on children, we need to make it meaningful for our school-based practice. The first way we are going to do this is in the next chapter. We are going to discuss the major policy that often governs our practice with homeless children and youth, the McKinney-Vento Homeless Assistance Act (MVA). The MVA is the overarching policy in America that addresses homelessness. There are very specific provisions which address school-based responses to homelessness that will frame our practice. As we move from understanding homelessness and its impact on children and youth to understanding how to address homelessness in our school-based practice, we must have a general understanding of the policy that governs what we do in schools for homeless children and youth.

Practice Takeaways

- Homelessness is a relatively new issue.
- The issue of child homelessness has only been studied for around 30 years.
- There is much inconsistency in who is worse: homeless children or their housed, but impoverished peers.
- Children and youth experiencing homelessness perform poorly academically.
- They have elevated rates of mental health problems.
- They have poor healthcare outcomes.
- Homeless children and youth have poor access to healthcare.
- Efforts have been made to clarify how homelessness impacts youth.
- Many studies focus on finding different types of homelessness.
- We can typologize homelessness in several ways: by length of time homeless, number of times homeless, or through outcomes.
- Ecological-systems perspectives allow for us to organize how people become and stay homeless.

3

The McKinney-Vento Act and School-Based Practice

"Yet we are the movers and shakers
Of the world for ever, it seems."

—Arthur O'Shaughnessy

What Is the McKinney-Vento Homeless Assistance Act?

The first two chapters of this book deal with how to think about homelessness and give us a solid foundation and understanding of the issue. A common question that could be brought up in chapter 2 is that if we know experiencing homelessness can lead to severe negative outcomes, what do we do about it? This chapter starts us on our journey to answering that question. Much of our school-based practice with homeless children will revolve around implementing a policy designed to help these children obtain equal educational opportunity. Lots of laws and policies address homelessness in America—panhandling precedents, loitering legislation, construction codes (especially in the case of shelter locations), and so on. However, *the* federal policy on homelessness in America for us as school-based practitioners is the McKinney-Vento Homeless Assistance Act (MVA).

This policy gives overarching guidance on addressing homelessness overall in the country. The MVA provides for a myriad of programs ranging from shelter funding to veterans' work programs but arguably, it is most known since its inception for its educational provisions. The MVA as a whole funds, oversees, or creates various programs and agencies that address homelessness in America. For example, the Continuum of Care programs, emergency shelter funding, and the Interagency Council on Homelessness all come from the policy. Although the MVA as a whole influences different aspects of the nation's response to homelessness, this book is about school-based practice with homeless children and youth, so we will primarily focus on the educational provisions of the policy for this and the next chapter. Therefore when we reference the MVA in the next chapters, we are doing so with an eye on the educational provisions as they relate to our school-based practice.

The policy was enacted in 1987 as the Stewart B. McKinney Act and several provisions were designed to remove the administrative barriers homeless children typically faced when trying to enroll and attend school. Even after several reauthorizations, amendments, expansion, and renaming, one of the primary goals for the MVA remains the same: uphold the right to equal educational opportunity. This chapter describes the MVA and its relationship to school-based practitioners, conceptualization of the policy, and finally how provisions fit into that conceptualization. Basically, this chapter sketches a summary of significant statutes in order to support school social workers and related-services specialists and professionals serving homeless children and youth. It does this in two ways: one, by equipping us with an understanding of our importance in implementing policy through practice, and two, by giving us a conceptually organized list of the major provisions the MVA provides. As we move from *thinking* about homelessness to *practicing* with those experiencing homelessness, our understanding of the MVA and its provisions will be an important foundation to support our efforts. An important thing to note about this chapter is that is a general guide to the policy and provisions. It is not meant to be legal advice, just a guide. Also, the MVA advocates that we as practitioners take a case-by-case approach to the facilitation of provisions. We should examine the details of each case before we make an MVA-related decision. Again, this chapter is a guide and not meant to replace legal counsel and advice.

Foundational Knowledge of the McKinney-Vento Homeless Assistance Act (MVA)

Purpose of the Policy

The purpose of the MVA is to uphold the right to educational opportunity for homeless children (42 U.S.C. 11431 *et seq.*). For us as school-based practitioners, this means getting homeless kids in school and keeping them enrolled. This also means offering a stabilized and "normal" school experience. According to the law, homeless children have the right to the entire school experience any nonhomeless child would have under normal circumstances (42 U.S.C. §11434A(1)). This means we have to continually ask ourselves, "if this student were not homeless, could they do this or would this be a problem?" For example, if there are attendance requirements to be on a sports team and the child has missed too many days of school because of her or his homeless situation, we would still allow the child to play (42 U.S.C. §11434A(1)). We must provide homeless students with every opportunity to succeed, and we do this by eliminating the barriers to equal and normal educational opportunity (42 U.S.C. §§11432(g) (1)(I), (g)(7).

Who Is Eligible for Services?

In the first chapter we went over the federal definition of homelessness. We started with the narrower Department of Housing and Urban Development definition and moved to the more inclusive Department of Education description. As stated in chapter 1, we would come back to the idea of fixed, regular, and adequate nighttime residence. It is how the MVA defines who is eligible for services (42 U.S.C. §11434A(2)(A)). What can be problematic about this is that the MVA does not give us specific definitions of fixed, regular, and adequate. We can start to address the ambiguity by examining the general definitions of what these terms mean. *Fixed* indicates that something is relatively permanent and will not change. If someone lacks a fixed living situation, it would be temporary and non-permanent. *Regular* means something is standard, normal, and consistently used, so its opposite would be inconsistent or abnormal. Finally, *adequate* means sufficient for the need; its antonyms would be *inadequate* or *deficient*. So for our general definition of who is homeless, it would be someone who lives in a temporary, consistently changing, and inadequate or deficient place to stay.

Now that we have a general idea of who is eligible for services, we can take some time to discuss specific situations the MVA outlines as experiences of homelessness. In comparison to other definitions, the MVA's is relatively broad and includes many different situations that other agencies, such as HUD, would not define as homeless. For example, families who are living with relatives or other friends could be considered homeless under the MVA (42 U.S.C. §11434A(2)(B)(i), but not in other definitions. This housing situation, called *doubling up*, is interesting because sometimes families choose to share housing in a fixed, regular, and sufficient way because of cultural reasons or convenience. To take this into account, the MVA requires us to examine each situation of homelessness or potential homelessness on an individual case-by-case basis. We must remember to look at the context of the situation as we identify children for services.

Continuing our look at different situations the policy considers homeless, it seems kind of obvious that if a child is living in a homeless shelter, he or she is homeless. This is true because most shelters are designed to be temporary (lacking fixed and regularity) in nature, but transitional housing programs are a little more permanent. Yet if a child resides at one of these programs they are also included in the definition and entitled to the provisions of the MVA (42 U.S.C. §11434A(2)(B)(i)). In addition, migrant children are included if they lack fixed, regular, and sufficient nighttime residence (42 U.S.C. §11434A(2)(b)(iv)). Because of Plyler v. Doe, 457 U.S. 202, undocumented immigrant students have the same rights to educational opportunity, and if they meet the criteria for homelessness, they too are eligible for services. Finally, children awaiting foster care placements are eligible for services (42 U.S.C. §11434A(2)(B)(i)).

School-Based Practitioners and MVA Implementation: Homeless Liaisons

Now that we have talked about who is eligible for MVA provisions, we must ask ourselves, how does it apply to school social work and related-services practice? Usually when we talk about our school-based practice with homeless children and youth, it almost always seems that we are talking about acting or serving as a "homeless liaison." Officially, liaisons are responsible for ensuring homeless children are able to enroll and attend school, for providing referrals to outside agencies for homeless families and for advocating for upholding the right to educational opportunity (42 U.S.C. §11432(g)(1)(J) (ii)). The main duties of this position include identifying homeless children for services, improving awareness both in and outside of the school, and serving as an advocate for school-aged children experiencing homelessness (42 U.S.C. §11432(g)(1)(J)(ii)). This position is an MVA-mandated requirement (42 U.S.C. §11432(g)(1)(J)(ii)) for educational agencies. And often, the responsibilities of a liaison are realized through our efforts in practicing with homeless children and youth.

Along those lines, our practice with these children and youth frequently revolves around implementing the provisions of the MVA to uphold the right to equal educational opportunities, meaning that policy implementation and school social work practice with homeless children and youth are closely related (Jozefowicz-Simbeni & Israel, 2006). Accordingly, the actions and perceptions of school social workers and related-services personnel underpin the implementation of the MVA. We have to understand that policies have goals and intended consequences for their provisions, and how the provisions are carried out depends on how we think of both the policy and the problem being addressed (Spillane et al., 2002). So thought and understanding of a problem influence how a policy is implemented (Spillane, 2000)— how we think influences how we act. For us, this means that how we think about policy provisions and homelessness in our service area will impact how we practice.

Thinking about the MVA

When we think, practice, evaluate, or really do anything else regarding a policy, we need to look at the "active ingredients" for a legislation. This means that we need to focus on what is actually the driving force or ideas behind a policy. I advocate that we should think about how we implement the MVA as the sum of three different aspects of the policy. These three areas, preparation, accessibility, and collaboration, provide us a clear conceptualization for all of the different provisions offered (Canfield, Teasley, Abell, & Randolph, 2012). It also allows us to organize and clarify our practice tasks with school-aged homeless youth. This conceptualization does have some initial empirical support (Canfield, Teasley, Abell, & Randolph, 2012) and can serve as a basis for our understanding and thought on the policy. But more importantly, it serves as a foundation for how we should approach school-based practice with homeless children and youth.

Preparation

The first aspect of MVA implementation is preparation. In order for us to implement the MVA and its provisions in practice, our service areas must have a plan to prepare for the needs of homeless children (Canfield et al., 2012). We need to be ready to address the myriad of needs, barriers, and facilitators our clients face. We also have to make sure other people in our schools know this as well. So our practice tasks may include education for the other professionals at our school. Because secretaries often serve as gate-keepers to the school, informing them about the policy and what to look for when identifying homeless children may help to facilitate identification. As we practice, we must prepare our school district for the needs of homeless

---

children. Everyone involved must know their role and understand that each system within a school has an important impact in providing homeless children and youth educational opportunities (Haber & Toro, 2004; Kilmer, Cook, Cursto, Strater, & Haber, 2012). Furthermore, we must prepare the outside community for the needs of homeless children (Altshuler, 2003). Thinking back to systems theory, we must remember that both systems in and out of the school will impact our practice and our ability to serve homeless children and youth.

Accessibility

The next concept of MVA implementation is the idea of accessibility. School accessibility is the major intent of the MVA and the major provisions within the policy address accessibility in many ways. The policy improves accessibility through requiring schools to adjust enrollment procedures to help children enroll or maintain enrollment in school, thus reducing barriers a school-aged child experiencing homeless faces (Biggar, 2001; Jozefowicz-Simbeni & Israel, 2006; Jullianelle & Foscarinis, 2003). Educational agencies must allow homeless children to enroll in school and participate fully in all activities associated with being a student in our service area (42 U.S.C.§11432(g)(1) (I), (g)(7)).

When we think of accessibility, we should think of it in five ways: geographically, economically, administratively, cognitively, and psychosocially. This is based off of Bertrand, Hardee, Magnani, and Angle's (1995) description of accessibility in their work examining access for a set of programs and services. So for those of us working with homeless children and youth in school settings, accessibility is the extent that our service area makes itself and educational opportunities available to children experiencing homelessness through geographic, economic, administrative, cognitive, and psychosocial means (Canfield, Teasley, Abell, & Randolph, 2012).

The Key Accessibility Provisions

The five-point definition of accessibility provides us with a good framework to examine specific provisions of the MVA. This is particularly important because these provisions often serve as the basis of many interventions in our practice. If you work with homeless children, you probably are already familiar with many of the provisions, but it always helps to have a good review. This part of the chapter is a guide and a cheat sheet for the policy; however, it is not meant to serve as a replacement for legal counsel.

Geographical Accessibility

Our understanding of geographical accessibility surrounds two key areas: the school of origin and transportation. The school of origin is the school that the child attended during his or her last experience of permanent housing, but in the case of chronic homelessness, it is the last school in which the student was (42 U.S.C. §11432(g)(3)(G)). The MVA wants educational agencies to keep students in their school of origin if at all possible. This may mean that if a child's homeless experience takes her or him to a different district's geographical boundaries, the child is still able to remain enrolled in the original district. Furthermore, homeless children and youth have the right to stay enrolled in the same building because this promotes stability. Even if a child moves to a nearby state, the policy advises us that the student should remain in the same school if it is feasible. Our default approach should be to keep the child in the same school, but if it is against the parents or guardians' wishes or keeping the child in the same school would be impossible, we may have to adjust our procedures. Like many provisions of the policy, we have to take a case-by-case look at the situation.

Transportation is often cited as a major barrier for homeless children and youth as they pursue educational opportunity (James & Lopez, 2003). The MVA stresses that school districts must remove transportation as a barrier to education (42 U.S.C. §§11432(g)(1)(I), (g)(7)). Educational agencies are required to provide transportation similar to what housed students receive as much as feasibly possible (42 U.S.C. §11432(g)(4)(A)), and if a parent or guardian requests it, the school has to provide transportation to the school of origin (42 U.S.C. §11432(g)(1)(J)(iii)). We will discuss funding for transportation in the collaboration section, but when it comes to accessibility and feasibility, we must examine feasible transportation in terms of the trip to school itself. The policy itself does not give any guidance on mileage or time limits on a trip to a school of origin, so we have to examine whether or not the length of a trip to school is harmful to each individual student's ability to achieve academically. A trip to school that may be appropriate for a high school student may not be acceptable for a first grader. Again, we must use the policy to guide us on our case-by-case decisions.

Economic Accessibility

The MVA strives to reduce barriers that prevent children and youth experiencing homelessness an equal and "normal" school experience. So if fees to participate in extra-curricular activities such as club dues or sports equipment

---

serve as a barrier to full participation in school, they must be waived (42 U.S.C.§§11432(g)(1)(I), (g)(7). In addition, The Child Nutrition and WIC Reauthorization Act of 2004 made it possible that any student whot is identified as homeless is automatically eligible for free school lunch.

Administrative Accessibility

We should think of administrative accessibility as getting rid of paperwork (in reality it is not so much getting *rid* of paperwork requirements, but more like making sure a child gets into the school and classes before everything is turned in). The policy requires immediate enrollment even if a child and/ or family cannot provide all of the documents that are usually needed (42 U.S.C. §11432(g)(3)(C)), meaning we need to focus on getting a child into school without delays because of administrative "paperwork." So things like residency requirements and age verification are waived (42 U.S.C. §11432(g) (3)(C)). Lack of immunization records also cannot prevent a homeless child from immediately enrolling and attending school (42 U.S.C.§11432(g)(3) (C). As part of getting a homeless child into school without delay, sometimes we may need to place them into a class and then adjust once we get their records. Once a student is admitted, the educational agency must contact the previous school to obtain records (42 U.S.C. §§11432(g)(3)(C), (D)). Schools may not need a parent's permission for obtaining records from the previous school because the Federal Education Rights and Privacy Act allows educational agencies to release records, without parental or guardian consent, when a student is transferring (20 U.S.C. §1232g). Again, our focus should be on removing all barriers to school enrollment that arise from experiencing homelessness.

Cognitive Accessibility

Homeless youth and their families must be aware of the policy and what it can do to help aid in educational opportunity attainment (42 U.S.C. §§11432(g) (6)(A)(i), (iv)). To do this, educational agencies uses liaisons to provide information in areas in which homeless families are known to live, such as shelters or soup kitchens (42 U.S.C. §11432(g)(6)(A)(v)). Homeless children and families must also be made aware that public charter schools have the same responsibilities that other schools have under the MVA. Also, if a child meets criteria to attend a skill-related public school (music, art, drama, etc.) he or she is covered by provisions of the MVA. Our efforts to improve awareness should be done to reduce or eliminate any stigma from being identified as homeless. Because the parents' wishes are so highly valued in carrying out the policy, ensuring they are knowledgeable about what the MVA can do is necessary.

Psychosocial Accessibility

As stated several times, the policy strives to provide equal and "normal" educational experiences for homeless children and youth. This means children and youth experiencing homelessness are allowed to fully participate in all school activities without stigma (42 U.S.C. §11434A(1)). This also means that homeless students can be subject to discipline, but we must be careful to not punish students for behavioral problems related to homelessness (42 U.S.C. §§11432(g)(1)(I), (g)(7)). A common example would be detentions or actions resulting from too many absences. If the absences are caused by homelessness, punishing the student for missing too much school would cause a barrier to continued enrollment for the homeless child. Finally, students cannot be separated because of homelessness (42 U.S.C.§11432(e)(3)(A)). We cannot allow homeless students to receive their education in places different than their peers. Except for a few exempted programs, homeless children and youth must receive their education in the same manner as their peers according to the MVA.

Collaboration

The final concept of MVA implementation is collaboration. It is a core idea of the MVA and important for us to remember as school social workers and related-services personnel. Schools are not social service agencies (Allen-Meares, 2010), and the needs of homeless school-aged children often fall outside the scope and purpose of a school. In the previous chapter, we went over two examples wherein situations outside of the school still impacted what happened inside the school. The MVA takes an approach to addressing the barriers homeless school children face by requiring schools to look to outside agencies for help. This is the main idea of collaboration in the MVA: working with outside entities to address the educational needs of homeless children (Canfield et al., 2012).

The provisions that describe collaboration focus on school social workers and other-related services professionals' work with three entities: parents, other school districts, and other agencies or programs that serve the homeless. In the accessibility section we discussed how important the parents are in making decisions in the best interest of the children we serve. This requires us to work with the parents to uphold the policy. We must do this in a way that creates an atmosphere through our practice to allow and encourage homeless children, youth, and their families to obtain and seek support and services.

A major hurdle to providing the transportation homeless children are entitled is determining who pays for it. The MVA states that if transportation is between two districts, they should figure out a way to split the cost and responsibility or split it equally between the two (42 U.S.C. §11432(g) (1)(J)(iii)). To settle disputes, the MVA requires that states establish procedures to resolve any issues between school districts (42 U.S.C. §11432(g) (1)(C)), but schools must make sure that the child is immediately enrolled (42 U.S.C. §11432(g)(3)(E)). This may require us to collaborate and network with other educational agencies to facilitate transportation. James and Lopez (2003) found that collaboration between educational agencies can be a major facilitator to providing comprehensive transportation services.

Schools have to work with other agencies such as shelters to ensure families are made aware of MVA provisions, but they may work with other agencies too. For example, schools may have to work with police in cases in which a homeless student may have run away from home. If abuse is suspected, mandatory reporting laws may require school social workers to contact proper authorities. The important thing to remember is that, as we discussed in previous chapters, homelessness does not occur in a vacuum. There is a constellation of different factors outside the school's control that impact outcomes, so it is necessary to work with other agencies, people, and systems that can impact a child experiencing homelessness.

Summary

This chapter provides a summary of the MVA and its provisions. In addition, we review a conceptualization of the policy by identifying the "active ingredients," the driving ideas behind what we do with the policy. Implementation of the MVA can be thought to be made up of three subareas: preparation, accessibility, and collaboration. Through these three areas, we are able to implement the purpose of the MVA, which is to uphold the right to equal educational opportunity. Again, this chapter is meant to be a general guide to the policy—the MVA itself advocates for a case-specific approach, and given the details of each case, interpretation could be different (this chapter should not replace legal counsel and advice). However, this chapter provides a good guideline and practice approach to the policy. In the next chapter, we will discuss how to take our knowledge of the policy gained here and use it in our practice to address the issues we discussed in chapter 2.

Important Provisions of the McKinney-Vento Act

- Purpose: uphold the right to educational opportunity for homeless children (42 U.S.C. 11431 et seq.)
- Homeless children have the right to the entire school experience any nonhomeless child would have under normal circumstances (42 U.S.C. §11434A(1)).
- Liaisons: responsible for ensuring homeless children are able to enroll and attend school, for providing referrals to outside agencies for homeless families, and for advocating for upholding the right to educational opportunity (42 U.S.C. §11432(g)(1)(J)(ii))
- Liaison duties: identify homeless children for services, improving awareness both in and outside of the school, and serving as an advocate for school-aged children experiencing homelessness (42 U.S.C. §11432(g)(1)(J)(ii))

Different Forms of Accessibility

Geographical Accessibility

- School of origin: school that child attended when permanently housed or the last school the student was enrolled in (42 U.S.C. §11432(g)(3)(G)).
- Districts must remove transportation as a barrier to education (42 U.S.C. §§11432(g)(1)(I), (g)(7)).
- Transportation similar to what housed students receive as much as feasibly possible (42 U.S.C. §11432(g)(4)(A)).
- Provide transportation to the school of origin when necessary (42 U.S.C. §11432(g)(1)(J)(iii)).

Economic Accessibility

- Fees must be waived (42 U.S.C.§§11432(g)(1)(I), (g)(7).

Administrative Accessibility

- The policy requires immediate enrollment (42 U.S.C. §11432(g)(3)(C)).
- Administrative requirements such as residency requirements and age verification are waived (42 U.S.C. §11432(g)(3)(C)).
- Immunization records can be waived (42 U.S.C.§11432(g) (3)(C).
- Previous school must be contacted to obtain records (42 U.S.C. §§11432(g)(3)(C), (D)).

Cognitive Accessibility

- Homeless families must be made aware of the policy and what it can do to help aid in educational opportunity attainment (42 U.S.C. §§11432(g)(6)(A)(i), (iv)).
- Liaisons must provide information in areas where homeless families are known to live, such as shelters or soup kitchens (42 U.S.C. §11432(g)(6)(A)(v)).

Psychosocial Accessibility

- Full participation in all school events must be granted without stigma (42 U.S.C. §11434A(1)).
- Do not punish students for behavioral problems related to homelessness (42 U.S.C. §§11432(g)(1)(I), (g)(7)).
- Students cannot be separated because of homelessness (42 U.S.C.§11432(e)(3)(A)).

Collaboration

- Districts must figure out a way to split the cost and responsibility or split it equally between the two (42 U.S.C. §11432(g)(1)(J)(iii)).
- MVA requires that states establish procedures to resolve any issues between school districts (42 U.S.C. §11432(g) (1)(C)).

4

███

The McKinney-Vento Act in School-Based Practice

"Unless someone like you cares a whole awful lot, nothing is
going to get better. It's not."

—*Dr. Seuss*

In the previous chapters we developed a foundation for understanding
homelessness and its impact on children and youth and then reviewed the
policy and provisions of the MVA. Those chapters provided an overview
and description of the issue and policy, but this chapter will discuss trans-
lating the legislation and using the provisions into practice. We will use the
information and illustrations in previous chapters to help provide concrete
examples of policy provisions in practice. To do this, we will go over how we
can implement preparation, accessibility, and collaboration to address barriers and facilitators in practice. Next, we will discuss what is known in the
literature about the MVA. Finally, we will discuss a way to assess perceived
implementation of the MVA in our service areas.

How the McKinney-Vento Homeless Assistance Act (MVA) Provisions Fit in Practice

Now that we have a solid foundation of what the MVA tells us about what
we need to do to help homeless children and youth, we need to start thinking about how this looks in practice. Many of you reading this may already
know how the provisions are carried out in your service area. So instead
of listing examples of how specific provisions can be implemented, we are
going to focus on providing examples and situations of the three domains of

implementation discussed in the previous chapter: preparation, accessibility, and collaboration. How we think about a policy impacts how we implement a policy (Spillane, 2000), so we should spend some time better understanding the mindset behind MVA implementation.

Preparation

Preparation is not necessarily rooted as firmly into MVA provisions as accessibility and collaboration. Preparation is more of a practice attitude and mindset rather than specific tasks. For example, preparation could be creating an atmosphere of cooperation across the faculty and staff in a service area. In some schools, this may be creating awareness and an environment in which a teacher who notices some "red-flag" behaviors or indicators of homelessness and knows what to do can get the student services. On top of this, creating an aware and united school will go a long a way in helping homeless students and facilitating the MVA. This is the core of preparation: making sure that all faculty and staff are aware of the MVA and what it can do for students.

Our ecological-systems perspective will help us prepare for the needs of homeless children. We need to make sure that every system knows their role in addressing homelessness (Reed-Victor & Pelco, 1999), especially in our schools. Haber & Toro (2004) tell us that in an ecological perspective, there are many different systems at play for those experiencing homelessness. For us as school-based practitioners, we need to recognize which systems are helping students and which are preventing educational attainment and then address them. In addition, we also need to prepare the community for the needs of homeless children. There are often systems in place in both the community and the school that can influence outcomes for homeless children (Berliner, 2009; Miller, 2009b). As we prepare for the needs of homeless children, we must remember to address as many systems as we can to improve the educational opportunities for children and youth experiencing homelessness.

Accessibility

Improving school accessibility is arguably one of the main tasks we complete when we serve homeless children and youth. Much of our practice involves carrying out the provisions of the MVA to achieve this goal. In the previous chapter we discussed what provisions in the policy address accessibility and how we can organize them. This section will go over how we can address a

---

couple common areas with the MVA in order to improve school accessibility for children and youth experiencing homelessness.

Transience

Transience is a major issue for homeless children and youth. Often homeless students move between living situations and schools, which causes much disruption to their educational experience. Improving stability is important in order to provide equal opportunities for school-aged homeless children to achieve academically (Bowman & Barksdale, 2004). The MVA provides several provisions that directly address transience. First, the provisions that deal with the school of origin are designed to promote stability. As a reminder, homeless children are allowed to remain in the same school even if their homeless housing situation takes them into another district ((42 U.S.C. §11432(g)(3)(G)). By addressing instability in the academic experience, we should therefore be providing better accessibility to education.

Identification

Many school social workers who practice with homeless children and youth will comment that identification is one of the most difficult aspects of the job. In order to spur identification, the MVA requires schools to improve the awareness of the policy and the rights afforded to homeless families. Schools and school-based practitioners can address problems associated with transience by providing information in shelters and other locales in which homeless families will be able to obtain knowledge ((42 U.S.C. §11432(g)(1)(J)(ii)). The MVA intentionally uses the liaison position to help schools find homeless children and youth ((42 U.S.C. §11432(g)(1)(J)(ii)).

Collaboration

The idea of collaboration in MVA implementation is really the lynchpin of our practice within the policy. Preparation is how we get ready to help homeless children and youth. Accessibility is our goal for the policy and practice. Collaboration is often how we achieve the goals of our practice and uphold the rights to educational opportunity. Oftentimes in our practice with homeless children and youth we will have to collaborate with other faculty and staff, outside agencies, and families to prepare for the needs of youth experiencing homelessness and to improve their access to educational opportunity.

Although we do not have empirical evidence that collaboration does improve accessibility and is needed to prepare schools for homeless children, there is literature that focuses on collaboration to help homeless children and youth. Although the definition of collaboration we used in chapter 3 focused on going outside of the school to help homeless children pursue educational opportunity, in this section we will also discuss the in-school collaboration tasks we can undertake.

In-School Tasks

School social work practice takes place in a host setting—social work is not the primary function of the school (Allen-Meares, 2010). Therefore it is necessary for us as school social workers and other related-service professionals to collaborate with others to support the basic purpose of the school. For our work with homeless children and youth, a good way to organize our collaboration tasks is by each of the different faculty and staff positions commonly found at a school.

Teachers

Teachers are obviously at the forefront of education and often have the most direct contact with students, so our tasks to collaborate with teachers should maximize this. How teachers perceive homelessness can be a major barrier or facilitator to our efforts (Kim, 2013; Powers-Costello & Swick, 2011). We can start by training teachers about what characteristics they can look for to aid in identifying homeless children. Oftentimes teachers will not have the opportunities to knowingly interact with homeless children, and this often leads to inaccurate perceptions of who are the homeless (Kim, 2013). Therefore we should take some effort to train teachers and address some misconceptions about homelessness (Kim, 2013) through education about some identifiable characteristics of their potentially homeless students. Some of the major traits teachers would be able to observe may be poor hygiene, poor attendance, consistent tardiness, children wearing the same clothes several days in a row, and a consistent lack of school supplies. This is particularly important because identification is both necessary for facilitating services, but it is also on the onus of the school ((42 U.S.C. 11431 *et seq.*).

Once we have identified a child, we should provide assistance, support, and guidance to teachers to make the classroom experience more accepting of homeless students, and thus provide equal educational opportunities

((42 U.S.C. 11431 *et seq.*). A good example of this would be to encourage teachers to adjust the requirements of some assignments. This sometimes subtle action may be a significant step teachers can make to help a homeless student. It also allows us to use our barriers and facilitators approach in practice. So accepting a hand-written paper from a homeless child rather than a typed one would not only be an accommodation in class, but it also addresses a potential barrier in computer access. Similarly, in-class discipline can also be adjusted. We need to encourage teachers to avoid punishing homeless children and youth for factors beyond their control. For example, we should discourage disciplining homeless students for something like lacking supplies and possibly use understanding and discretion for other situations such as when a homeless child steals something like food. Finally, we should encourage teachers to make every effort to plan for a student to easily assimilate into a new classroom environment. This may be something as simple as providing a class schedule or even preparing supplies for the student.

Vignette: Working with Teachers and Homeless Students

A school social worker friend told me a story about working with a teacher regarding a homeless student. The child's father was in prison and the mother was a hardcore drug user and would often leave the kid alone for days when she needed her fix. The child moved around as the mom did and they bounced between foster care and their relatives' houses often. Because of foster care involvement, the child was identified for MVA services and was able to remain in the same class even when he changed residence.

In his class, the teacher assigned a timeline project about the student's life and family and he did not want to do it. The teacher was in communication with the school social worker and knew the child was identified as homeless and was receiving MVA services. She gave the child supplies and extra time for the student to complete the assignment. When he still refused to do it, she got furious and took his recess away.

The social worker knew there was something more to the story. In one of their sessions, the student said he did not want to write about all the times his mom went away or talk about the date his dad went to prison. The school social worker helped the student come up with a "timeline" to complete the project that completed the purpose of the assignment, but also left out the sensitive information the child did not want to share.

This is a good example of some of the extra work we may need to undertake when we collaborate with teachers to implement the MVA and more importantly advocate and help students experiencing homelessness obtain education. In this example, the teacher cared and understood some of the challenges of experiencing homelessness, but struggled to think of the factors outside of time and supplies that can affect whether and how a student completes the assignment. In this case, a timeline of family events may be a good assignment for the vast majority of students, but not necessarily for ones experiencing homelessness.

Administrators

It is a little clearer which provisions of the MVA we can use to help support administration. Often, we will have to remind administrators that homeless children and youth have the right to immediately enroll or maintain enrollment at a school (42 U.S.C. §11432(g)(3)(E)). Anecdotally, this is one of the most common barriers to school-based practice with homeless youth that arises as we collaborate with administrators. We often need to advocate for students experiencing homelessness through reminding school administrators what the MVA provides to homeless children.

We also need to encourage and foster collaboration between administration of our service area and the administration of other educational entities. Locally, this will help to expedite enrollment processes between schools. If administrators have agreements in place to share transportation or transfer records, valuable time can be saved. At a state level, school administrators will need to interact with officials in the event of a dispute (42 U.S.C. §11432(g)(1)(C)). Along these lines, we will have to support and encourage administration to work together with other district employees to resolve any conflict that arises in our attempts to facilitate the MVA and its provisions. Finally, we need to make sure that administration is aware of any "red flag" indicators that a child may be homeless. Common indicators could be referrals for truancy or poor attendance, or behavior problems such as sleeping in class. Although these behaviors do not always indicate that a child is experiencing homelessness, they could warrant investigation into the matter.

School Secretaries and Enrollment Personnel

Creating awareness and training faculty and administration may be a great aid to helping homeless students, but if we neglect to include the gatekeepers of the school in our collaboration we will fail in our efforts to carry out the MVA before we start. Gatekeepers to the school, often school secretaries, must be aware of telltale signs of homelessness as families enroll their children into school. A good way to do this is in training is to go over common phrases families and children may use when enrolling. When filling out forms with an address a homeless family may say something along the lines of, "I can't remember, it is new," or use the address of a shelter. We need to also make sure that school secretaries and enrollment personnel are aware of the various experiences that can be considered homeless according to MVA definitions. We cannot assume that everyone knows all of the different ways a family or child could be considered homeless. Typically, we think of the homeless as single males living in skid-row types of locales (Mickelson & Yon, 1995) or we may picture a family living in a car—not a family staying with relatives temporarily. Once a family and student are identified as needing homeless services, several subtle actions can make a big difference in getting a child enrolled. Offering assistance in filling out forms or giving privacy to go over enrollment documentation can make family feel welcome. Along these lines, school secretaries and enrollment personnel must be able to describe the provisions and rights available to a homeless family.

School secretaries can be instrumental in adding stability if a homeless child does have to move schools by copying and documenting records to give to parents. This can help expedite the process of transferring between schools and provide a smooth transition. Finally, school secretaries and school social workers must maintain constant communication about homeless students. Secretaries should inform school social workers and related-services personnel when a potential homeless student has been identified. School social workers should also let secretaries know when a homeless child has been identified, to ensure that the student is not punished or disciplined for reasons beyond her or his control.

I was sitting in the front office of an elementary school waiting to speak to the principal about a research project. It was late in the school day and three girls walked into the office. They told the secretary they needed to sign into school. The secretary looked at them and asked them, "Why? The day is just about over. You only have 40 minutes left. Where have you been all day?"

The kids told the secretary how they had to wait for their mom or aunt to get home from work so they could get a ride. When their mom had to stay later they had to walk to their mom's friend's house and ask for a ride. When they could not get one there they just walked to school.

"Well OK, I'll do it for you guys this time," the secretary said as she callously rolled her eyes and grabbed the sign-in documents, "you really need to get here earlier though."

When the three girls left to go to their classes, she looked at me and said, "Can you believe that? Forty minutes left and they want to come to school?"

"Nope. I can't believe what I saw," I said speaking in double entendre. When my meeting started, this was an area that I brought up, without using names or talking about the specific situation, as an area in which collaboration could have been beneficial. Although the students may or may not have been homeless, they were experiencing some difficulties in getting to school. This was an obvious barrier to the children learning, so an intervention would be very beneficial. At the school level, training support staff and other members of the school to be cognizant of opportunities for referrals is an important and necessary intervention.

Nurse

School nurses also practice in a host setting. Similar to school social workers and other related-services personnel, their main focus is to support the primary purpose of the school, meaning our efforts to collaborate with them should keep this in mind. Like other personnel, nurses can help with identification, so understanding the characteristics of a homeless child would be important. However, nurses can be instrumental after identification has been made. Obtaining a medical history and previous records from other schools can be an important task in centralizing all student records. Nurses should be involved in determining plans for what happens if a student needs to return home in the event of illness.

Collaboration Outside of the School

As we discussed earlier, collaboration with agencies outside of the school is necessary in order to properly implement the MVA because schools are not inherently social service agencies (Allen-Meares, 2010). Our practice tasks may involve a lot of networking and cooperation between other agencies that routinely serve the homeless. It is often mentioned that there is a major disconnect between the outside community and the school when it comes to addressing poverty and homelessness (Altshuler, 2003; Berliner, 2009). In order to improve outcomes, especially academic ones, community involvement is key (Epstein & Sheldon, 2002). Any steps we can take to improve relationships or collaborate with other agencies will be very beneficial for our homeless children and youth.

Shelters and Other Agencies That Serve the Homeless

In order to carry out the provisions of the MVA, it is necessary for schools to be in contact with other agencies. School social workers and other related-services personnel can often be the conduit between the school and the outside world. Creating solid working relationships can facilitate our practice with homeless students. This is particularly important because many residing in shelters have low levels of awareness of MVA provisions (Hicks-Coolick, Burnside, Eaton & Peters, 2003). Collaboration can be a way to improve awareness, which will lead to increased identification for services. For example, shelter staff can notify school social workers when a family with school-aged children moves in. This type of relationship can be instrumental in identification, which is the responsibility of the educational agency ((42 U.S.C. 11431 *et seq.*). With schools being required to post notice of the rights to educational opportunity afforded by the MVA in places in which the homeless are known to congregate ((42 U.S.C. 11431 *et seq.*), consistent contact with homeless shelters can help with this process. Providing contact information or even training can be instrumental in identifying children.

Parents and Guardians

Parents and guardians are arguably the most important people to collaborate with in order to facilitate the MVA's provisions. Parenting and parental involvement have been shown to be an important mediator in how much homelessness impacts academics (Herbers et al., 2011; Miliotis, Sesma, & Masten, 1999). First and foremost, we need to ensure that parents understand the rights to educational opportunity. We need do this in a discrete and respectful way, but we must ensure that parents are fully informed. Along these lines, we need to let parents know how decisions are made. The policy defers to the best interest of the child ((42 U.S.C. 11431 *et seq.*) and this usually means that parents make this decision. Each service area will have its own policies and procedures, so it would be a good idea to keep the parents aware of these. Finally, we should make appropriate referrals as needed. Homeless parents often need much support in general (Willard & Kulinna, 2012), but even if we improve awareness about any problems or issues, they may not have the resources to address barriers (Yousey, Leake, Wdowik, & Janken, 2007). Our work with agencies outside of the school can help to provide a list of appropriate agencies to help families experiencing homelessness. Referrals can also be made within the school as well. Putting families in contact with the nurse or school secretary can help fill in gaps (e.g., no previous school records or immunizations) during the administration process.

Collaboration at a Glance

Administrators
- Familiarize the characteristics of homeless students.
- Facilitate collaboration between all of the different support staff and teachers.
- Build supportive networks with other schools.
- Network with state agencies about homelessness.
- Be aware of the rights provided to homeless children and families.

Secretaries/Enrollment Personnel
- Know and understand the characteristics of homeless students.
- Contact the liaison if homelessness is identified.

- Provide privacy for homeless parents.
- Provide guidance on completing the form.
- Make copies of school records for parents.
- Be familiar with the policies that address homelessness.

Nurse
- Obtain copies of medical records.
- Make plans in the event a homeless child must leave school early because of illness.
- Know and understand the characteristics of homeless students.
- Be familiar with the policies that address homelessness.

Teacher
- Know and understand the characteristics of homeless students.
- Contact the liaison if homelessness is identified.
- Adjust assignments to take into consideration some of the barriers homeless children face.
- Provide students with an information sheet about the class schedule and procedures.
- Provide supplies.
- Be familiar with the policies that address homelessness.

References: Altshuler, 2003; Berliner, 2009; Herbers et al., 2011; Kim, 2013; Mickelson & Yon, 1996; Powers-Costello & Swick, 2011; Willard & Kulinna, 2012; Yousey, Leake, Wdowik, & Janken, 2007

What Do We Know about the MVA?

The MVA is often cited in the literature on homeless children, but empirical studies are scarce. Our knowledge on the MVA is often anecdotal in nature and based on government reports. We can discuss the efficiency of the program, and some studies do this (Miller, 2009a). However, determining the effectiveness of the MVA has remained relatively elusive. The next section will discuss the literature on the MVA and what we know about it outside of the provisions.

Funding

Few people deny or disagree with the basic intent of the MVA, but many people feel that the policy is an unfunded mandate (Biggar, 2001). The policy provides for many valuable and necessary provisions, but the federal government has not backed up the intent with the necessary funding (Biggar, 2001). The way the MVA works in terms of funding, is that it is conditionally released to states. Only states that choose to receive funding are mandated to follow the provisions. The MVA requires states to set aside some funds to handle state-level MVA tasks, but requires state educational agencies to disburse subgrants to local education agencies. Many times subgrants are awarded on a competitive basis, though in some cases, other methods are used (funds are given out equally to every local agency, funding is determined by number of homeless children served, etc.). This leads to why many feel that the MVA is an unfunded mandate. State educational agencies are dealing with funding cuts and other austerity measures, so funds for additional services, such as the ones described in the MVA, may be reduced or eliminated. Next, a state may take funds, meaning that all schools receiving public funding (including charter schools) must abide by the policy, but then may not award funds to every district. So local education agencies are required to follow the rules of the policy but are not given the means to carry out the provisions.

With funding, one of the areas we can focus on is efficiency. In 2005-2006, we saw that 98% of children and youth identified as experiencing homelessness in subgranted educational agencies received support through the MVA (Miller, 2009a). However, this does not include the number of children who were not served because the educational agency did not receive a subgrant, but in later studies, 80% of the overall number of homeless students was considered to be served by MVA funds (National Center for Homeless Education, 2011).

Mandates Action

When we think of what we know and whether the MVA works, we often get stuck in examining quantitative analysis. We tend to only look at numbers: for example, how many children were served, was there a decrease in absences, or how are test scores? These are very important outcomes and markers of intended policy success, but we should also remember that the MVA shapes and morphs how we go about our practice with homeless children and youth (Miller, 2009a). For example, one of the major successes of the MVA is that it does *require* schools to act. The idea of immediate enrollment is thought to be a major accomplishment of the policy. In addition, before the enactment of the policy, the onus was on the family to provide documentation to enroll, whereas now the school must actively search for homeless students. Also, our tasks have been influenced by the policy man-dates of the MVA. The focus on providing equal opportunity has expanded from simply getting a child enrolled in school, to providing opportunities for children to participate fully in all school activities ((42 U.S.C. 11431 *et seq.*). So although we may not have the amount of quantitative evidence of policy effectiveness, we do have an understanding that the MVA, at the very least, has tremendously impact the way we practice. This, in a very important way, is a success for the policy.

Need to Constantly Assess Our Understanding of Homelessness

The MVA provides a unifying definition of homelessness for educational agencies to identify children for services. Before the 2002 reauthoriza-tion, there was much ambiguity and discrepancies between educational agencies (Miller, 2009a). This led to problems between districts when there was disagreement about who was homeless. The current defini-tion is an inclusive definition that includes many different situations of housing instability. However, the definition has changed over time as our understanding of the housing and shelter options families face when they become homeless improve and evolve. Because of our front-line role as school-based practitioners, we need to be acutely aware of the changing nature of homelessness. We need to continually examine situations that future definitions could include as an experience of homelessness. With the changing nature of how transience manifests itself in the lives our students, we need to be active in continually shaping the definition of homelessness.

Does the MVA Work?

Practitioners, researchers, policymakers, educators, and families tend to agree that a policy that addresses the barriers homeless children and youth face when pursuing education is necessary. Undoubtedly, the MVA is a needed policy in the American education system, and its provisions are valuable tools for school-based practitioners. But does it work? Does the policy actually help homeless children obtain equal educational oppor-tunity? At best, we do not know. Despite the importance of the legisla-tion, there is a dearth of literature on the effectiveness of the MVA. In fact, Hendricks and Barkley (2012) reported that the supervisor of the MVA program at the US Department of Education had not heard of any peer-reviewed evaluations.

Most of the literature on homelessness in general and the MVA specifically are descriptive in nature. The best articles on MVA evaluation simply describe the theoretical positive impacts of provisions or provide anecdotes of how school-based efforts have helped students. Hardly any systematic, quantitative state or nationwide studies exist on the efficacy of the program. One of the scant few quantitative studies examining the impact of the MVA focused on differences in academic achievement between schools receiving MVA funding and those that did not in one Southern state (Hendricks & Barkley, 2012). They found no significant differences in academic achievement between the funded and unfunded schools on end-of-grade test scores (Hendricks & Barkley, 2012). Other studies have estimated that the MVA improves attendance rates for homeless children by approximately 17% (Markward & Biros, 2001). In our effort to quantify the impact of the MVA, we have come to an interesting crossroad: what is success under the MVA?

The purpose of the policy is not to address *achievement*. Instead, it focuses on equal educational *opportunity*. This distinction raises interesting points in our evaluation efforts. First, what is equal educational opportunity, and does stabilizing the school experience count as equality? This is important to answer for our school-based practice. Although this may seem like a topic for researchers, it cuts to the core of our goals in practice. We must ask ourselves in our practice with homeless children and youth to define the overarching outcome of our interventions. As we use the MVA to provide stability in school attendance, does this mean we are providing educational opportunity? We have discussed how factors outside the school can impact systems within the school. Does this mean that failing to address outside elements indicates that we are not providing equal opportunity? How far can school-based interventions reach into the community? School social workers should be at the forefront of answering these questions because we are often the ones facilitating the policy. We should advocate at all levels, at the school, state, and nationally, for what we observe and understand in our practice with homeless children and youth.

Next, how much focus should we place on achievement? Because school is about education, academic outcomes are obviously very important. If a policy does not lead to improved academic outcomes, is it really important to a school? This question is important for practitioners in a host setting. Our interventions need to support the purpose of the school, which is education. The MVA provides much support to homeless children as they

School-Based Practice with Homelessness

pursue education, but if they are not successful in their education, it may indicate that the policy is insufficiently addressing the true needs of homeless children (Hendricks & Barkley, 2012). We know the policy is needed, but does it truly address the problem of homelessness and its effect on education?

So where do we start when it comes to evaluating the MVA in practice? I think at the macro level at least. Biggar (2001) provides three excellent criteria for us to evaluate the MVA: effectiveness, equity, and efficiency. These highlight very important challenges for practitioners. We cannot forget that policy decisions at a macro level will impact our micro-level practice. Biggar (2001) contends that the MVA is not truly effective because of noncompliance at the federal and state level. The federal and state governments do not provide timely and adequate funds to truly carry out the principles of the policy. Policies are only effective if they have "teeth," meaning that a policy must have a mechanism to carry out and enforce the provisions. In the case of transportation, the MVA requires that it be provided to homeless students, but does not necessarily provide or require additional funding to carry this out. Next is the equity of the policy. Because states must apply for funding (42 U.S.C. 11431 *et seq.*), MVA funds are not equally distributed. Furthermore, states decide how to dole out money to schools. In some states, funding is competitive, meaning that some schools do not receive funds. This means that some homeless students receive less support than homeless students in a different district. Other states may divide funding equally across districts without regard to need. So some districts may be able to spend more per homeless students than others. To put this in perspective, only 4% of school districts nationwide actually receive funding through the MVA, which means that only around 37% of homeless children actually receive services through the policy (Duffield & Lovell, 2008), which is different than what other agencies have found (National Center for Homeless Education, 2011). Finally, efficiency is the last aspect Biggar (2001) used to assess the policy. Factors that could improve MVA efficiency are indirect (Biggar, 2001). As we know, experiencing homelessness includes many different systems that impact and influence outcomes, and homelessness does not occur in schools. The educational provisions of the MVA only address one area of a homeless child's experience. Furthermore, no longitudinal studies on the effectiveness of the MVA exist, so we do not know if the MVA's provisions help prevent homeless children from becoming homeless adults.

What Can School-Based Practitioners Do?

This criticism is not to say that the policy is worthless, but that we truly need to know more about the MVA. School-based practitioners are in a prime spot to make meaningful macro-level changes to the policy. We must leverage our knowledge of what we see in practice, what we see as challenges and supports, and what we know of how the provisions are facilitated into improved policy for homeless children and youth. We then must support this with empirical knowledge on the effectiveness of the policy.

At the micro levels of school-based practice, we can take several steps to improve facilitation of the policy provisions. School social workers are uniquely positioned within a school to help children and youth experiencing homelessness. Through our understanding of homelessness, we know that homeless students are in need of other supports in addition to educational assistance (Davey, Penuel, Allison-Tant, & Rosner, 2000). School social workers and related-services personnel can provide many efforts to address the barriers homeless children face when obtaining an education in the context of facilitating the provisions of the MVA. These efforts can include advocacy, collaboration, improving awareness, improving identification of children for services, and other challenges to both MVA implementation and educational opportunities for school-aged children experiencing homelessness.

Evaluation and Assessment

Measuring the MVA

There is one measure that was specifically designed to measure perceived implementation of the MVA. It is the McKinney-Vento Act Implementation Scale (MVAIS) and was designed for practitioners to use in their service areas (Canfield et al., 2012). It has been used in over 10 states and has been validated in three separate studies. Yes, I know it is something I developed and this may seem like a shameless plug, but that means one really important thing: it is free to use (as long as you cite it) in your practice and service area. You are free to use it in needs assessments, grant applications, and even research studies if you wish, again, as long as you properly cite the validation study. This section is going to describe the structure of the MVAIS, why it is good to use, and how we can use it in our practice.

Structure of the MVAIS

The MVAIS is a 26-item rapid assessment instrument that measures perceived MVA implementation in three different domains. These domains reflect the three concepts of the MVA we discussed in the previous chapter: preparation, accessibility, and collaboration. Each of the 26 items is on a five-point Likert-type scale that ranges from "Strongly Disagree" to "Strongly Agree." The items of the MVAIS all correspond to a specific provision or part of the policy. For example, item number 14 asks, "How much do you agree with the following statements: My service area's policies and procedures allow a student who became homeless in the middle of a school year to remain enrolled in the same school even if the student moved out of the service area." This item is about letting homeless children stay enrolled in their school of origin (42 U.S.C. §11432(g)(3)(G). Another example is item 22, which is "How much do you agree with the following statements: My service area consistently: Contacts homeless shelters on behalf of homeless children," and is taken from provisions in the MVA that require educational agencies to collaborate with outside agencies to improve awareness of educational rights (42 U.S.C. §11432(g) et sequentia). The 26 items are divided up into four different sections. The first section is designed to measure preparation and includes items 1 through 5. Accessibility has two separate sections. The first section uses items 6 to 13 and the second section uses items 14 to 19. The final seven items (items 20–26) are designed to measure perceived collaboration.

How We Know the MVAIS Is Valid and Reliable

The MVAIS has actually gone through three separate psychometric validation studies to show that it is a sound instrument, starting with Canfield et al. in 2012. Psychometric studies usually focus on two different areas: validity and reliability. Validity is what it sounds like; it examines whether the measure is credible (Abell, Springer, & Kamata, 2009). We determine validity in five ways: face, content, factorial, construct, and criterion (Abell, Springer, & Kamata, 2009). Reliability is also what we think of it to be. We examine whether a scale is consistently measuring the same concept usually by examining Cronbach's alpha, a statistic that measures how well the items measure the same thing, also known as internal consistency. The MVAIS has been shown across these three studies to be a valid and reliable instrument.

Validity

There are five types of validity that we discuss: face, content, factor, construct, and criterion. During the first validation study, many of the people who responded would tell us that it looked like we had been researching the MVA. This means that, on its face, the MVAIS looks like it measures perceptions of MVA implementation. But before we even handed out the MVAIS to practitioners, experts in school social work, education, and psychometric measurement reviewed the items to make sure the content measured the notions of MVA implementation. Thinking that MVA implementation is made up of preparation, accessibility, and collaboration is statistically sound. We found that the three-factor structure of preparation, accessibility, and collaboration had appropriate fit through a confirmatory factor analysis. We used five different fit indices (χ^2/df ration, Tucker-Lewis Index, comparative fit index, root mean square error of approximation, and standardized root mean square residual) to show that the structure of the three concepts making up implementation appropriately fit our statistical findings. In the first study, we were able to show that the different sections of the MVAIS appropriately measure the intended construct through using single-items directly asking the intended concept. The final form of validity criterion has not been obtained because there is no other measure that can serve as a comparison. For example, if we were developing a self-esteem scale we could compare it to scores of the Rosenberg Self-Esteem Scale to get criterion validity. Once another metric of MVA implementation is created, we can compare the scores to determine criterion validity.

Reliability

All three validation studies used Chronbach's alpha to determine reliability. This is a measure of internal consistency that ranges from 0 to 1. Scores closer to 1 are preferred because this indicates that the items that make up a concept are measuring the same thing. According to Abell et al. (2009), we want our alpha scores to be above .8 to show that we have high reliability. We achieved this in all three studies. Items one through five (preparation) had an alpha score that ranged from .857 to .906, indicating high levels of reliability. Next, accessibility (items 6–19) had scores of .887 to .906. Finally, collaboration, made up of items 20 to 26, had high levels of internal consistency (alpha scores ranged from .917 to .941).

How Can We Use the MVAIS in Practice?

Now that we discussed the statistical foundation of the MVAIS, we can move on to a much more exciting topic: How can we use the MVAIS in practice? Or better yet, how can we use the MVAIS in our practice tasks while working with homeless children and youth? We can start by discussing how to use the MVAIS itself. Each of three subscales, preparation, accessibility, and collaboration, has items on the same Likert-scale. We can attach numbers to scoring possibilities by assigning a score of one if a person selects "Strongly Disagree" and up to five if someone selects "Strongly Agree." By assigning numbers to responses, we are able to add or average scores together.

If we just want to get a general idea of how well our service area perceives MVA implementation or its three subscales, preparation, accessibility, or collaboration, we can just add the scores together. For example if we want to see how well our area is collaborating with outside agencies, we can just add items 20 to 26 together. If we wanted perceived implementation overall, we would add all the items together. But if we want to compare scores, we should average the scale scores. So if we wanted to compare how well our school is preparing to how well we are collaborating, averaging the scores is the way to go. This is because the three subscales have a differing number of items. Preparation has five and collaboration has seven. If we added them together, preparation would have a range of 5 to 25, whereas collaboration would have a range of 7 to 35. All of these numbers are already making it confusing, so standardizing scores will help. Because each item has five possible choices, the scores can range from one to five. Averaging scores together keeps it at that scale and makes comparisons easy to make. Whether we choose to add the scores together or calculate averages, higher scores for the MVAIS indicate higher levels of perceived implementation.

Once we have decided how we will score responses, the MVAIS has great utility in needs assessments. It can tell us the general level of MVA implementation perceptions in our school as well as provide indicators of perceived preparation, accessibility, and collaboration. We will be able to highlight where our service area may be strong in addressing homelessness but also draw attention to areas for improvement. The MVAIS has been used in both traditional paper and pen formats and as an online email survey.

Ideally, the MVAIS would be used by school social workers and related-services personnel in several ways. First, it should be used in needs assessments. The tool lets us examine areas in which more focus may be needed and it may allow us to find out who we may need to focus our efforts on. Next, we should use it as proof of our efficacy, especially in times when we provide training and professional development/continuing educational opportunities within our service areas. Showing increases in scores would be beneficial and provide empirical evidence that perceptions of policy implementation are increasing through our efforts. Next, we can use the MVAIS to help with policy facilitation fidelity. This means that the MVAIS is a tool that will allow us to gain an understanding of whether we are implementing the policy as close to the intent as possible. Because the items of the instrument were taken directly from the policy itself, the MVAIS is a valid tool to measure the provisions of the policy. Finally, be encouraged to find different ways to use the measure in your practice. The MVAIS has been included in this chapter to provide another tool that you as practitioners can use as you see fit.

The McKinney-Vento Act Implementation Scale

The next set of questions is about policies and procedures regarding services for homeless children in your service area. Please read the statements on the left and circle the number that best represents your view on the scale provided.

In your opinion, how much do you agree with the following statements about your service area?	Strongly Disagree	Somewhat Disagree	Neutral	Somewhat Agree	Strongly Agree
1. The state in which I work has policy and procedures for working with homeless children and youth.	1	2	3	4	5
2. The policies and procedures for working with homeless children are available to employees in my service area.	1	2	3	4	5
3. Policies and procedures for working with homeless children are always accessible in my service area.	1	2	3	4	5
4. There are policies and procedures in my service area for reducing the stigma of homelessness.	1	2	3	4	5
5. Policies and procedures in my service area for practice with homeless children and youth are easily accessible.	1	2	3	4	5

Considering your service area's policies and procedures, how much do you agree with the following statements?	Strongly Disagree	Somewhat Disagree	Neutral	Somewhat Agree	Strongly Agree
It is easy for a homeless child in my service area to:					
6. Enroll in school	1	2	3	4	5
7. Enroll in school without proof of residency	1	2	3	4	5
8. Enroll in school without proof of immunization	1	2	3	4	5
9. Enroll in school without previous school records	1	2	3	4	5
10. Enroll in school without paying school fees in full	1	2	3	4	5
11. Participate in extra-curricular activities without paying fess	1	2	3	4	5
12. Obtain school supplies	1	2	3	4	5
13. Obtain reliable transportation	1	2	3	4	5

How much do you agree with the following statements?	Strongly Disagree	Somewhat Disagree	Neutral	Somewhat Agree	Strongly Agree
14. My service area's policies and procedures allow a student who became homeless in the middle of a school year to remain enrolled in the same school even if the student moved out of the service area.	1	2	3	4	5
15. My service area has someone assigned to locate homeless children and their families for school enrollment.	1	2	3	4	5
16. My service area has a policy or procedure to place information at homeless shelters, transitional houses, or other areas where the homeless congregate.	1	2	3	4	5
17. My service area provides counseling services for homeless children.	1	2	3	4	5
18. My service area provides psychosocial resources for children experiencing homelessness	1	2	3	4	5
19. My service area provides resources for children to reduce the stigma of being homeless while attending school.	1	2	3	4	5
My service area consistently:					
20. Contacts other agencies on behalf of homeless children	1	2	3	4	5
21. Utilizes other agencies to provide services for homeless children	1	2	3	4	5
22. Contacts homeless shelters on behalf of homeless children	1	2	3	4	5
23. Utilizes homeless shelter resources to aid homeless children	1	2	3	4	5
24. Contacts other school social workers regarding homeless children	1	2	3	4	5
25. Contacts parents of homeless children	1	2	3	4	5
26. Involves parents in making decisions for a homeless child	1	2	3	4	5

Canfield, J., Teasley, M., Abell, N., & Randolph, K. (2012). Validating a McKinney-Vento Act Implementation Scale. *Research on Social Work Practice, 22*, 410–419.

Summary

The MVA is an important policy in our school-based practice with children and youth experiencing homelessness. Our empirical knowledge on the effects of the policy may be limited, but we are starting to better understand how the policy plays out in practice. This chapter provided a few examples to ground our knowledge of the policy into real-world practice. We learned some tips about how to collaborate within the school and with outside agencies. We broadly went over the literature on the MVA, and discussed a valuable tool that will allow us to assess and evaluate our service area. School social workers and related-services personnel play a vital role in facilitating the MVA and its provisions, and should be at the forefront as the policy continues to evolve to address the ever-changing needs of homeless children and youth.

The next chapter focuses on a practice perspective for school social workers and other related services professionals. This perspective is developed out of our foundational knowledge on homelessness and what the policy provides. We are going to focus on the aspects of homelessness, the school, the community, and the individual that either help homeless children and youth obtain equal educational opportunity or prevent academic attainment.

Practice Takeaways

- Much of our practice will be carrying out the provisions of the MVA.
- We should organize our thoughts on the MVA in three ways: preparation, accessibility, and collaboration.
- Preparation is a mindset. We should make sure our schools and communities are ready for the needs of homeless children.
- Accessibility is addressed directly by the MVA.
- The MVA aims to improve educational opportunity by increasing accessibility.
- Collaboration should occur both inside and outside of the school.
- Our knowledge of the MVA is limited to descriptions.
- School social workers and other related-services personnel should take a lead in determining what outcomes are needed.
- We can measure perceived implementation with the McKinney-Vento Act Implementation Scale.

5

██ ██ ██

Barriers and Facilitators

A Practice Approach

"New knowledge is the most valuable commodity on earth. The
more truth we have to work with, the richer we become."

—*Kurt Vonnegut*

I play a game on the first day of a new class to help the students get to know
me a little better. It is called the "hot seat" and is a common game used in
group therapy. Everyone in the class is allowed to ask me any question they
want and I will always answer truthfully, or if I choose, I may decline to
answer and "pass." The students usually start with questions about me: my
favorite color (blue), my hobbies (I play hockey and read comic books, lots
of comic books), my favorite comic book (Chew), and so on. Invariably, they
then start asking about social work. Specifically, they ask what was my best
experience, worst experience, and sometimes most meaningful experience.
I always tell the same stories: My best experience was getting to drive a guy
to his first permanent home in over 10 years, doing the apartment inspection
with him, and then hearing the click of the lock when I left (if you've ever
worked with folks who have been homeless, incarcerated, or both, you will
know the significance of being able to lock a door). My worst experience will
come up a little later on in the chapter. But my most meaningful experience,
though, can help us frame a solid practice approach to our work with homeless children and youth.

I was an MSW intern at a transitional housing facility that had a small
basketball court for the kids to play on. It was a really nice setup for the kids

to shoot hoops, but there was no actual hoop for the ball to go through. So if you can imagine a nice, smooth, level asphalt playing space with a very high quality backboard attached to a sturdy and cemented pole, missing the one thing that was needed to actually play a game. This setup tantalized the kids with the fanciful, but ultimately deceitful hope of playing basketball. The kids would shoot pretending there was a hoop or just bounce the ball, but it really wasn't the same. I remember thinking how apropos—these children had the tools and potential, but there always seemed to be one glaring barrier that prevented them from success.

And as kids tend to do, they got bored and stopped playing on the court and really just stopped coming outside—the kids needed to be active and have some sort of normal childhood experience. So I took the responsibility of finding solutions to get the kids playing outside again. My first thought was to get the city parks and recreation department to give the kids waivers to participate in some of the sports programs. I then thought of getting some of the local university athletic departments to hold a camp for the kids. I even considered writing or calling some of the local professional sports teams to donate equipment and/or run a camp, among the other creative and imaginative ideas young interns tend to dream. My goal was to be resourceful while addressing a real need. During lunch about a week or so after I started brainstorming ways to solve the problem of getting homeless kids active, I spoke to the other intern, Dave, about what was going on and how I was struggling to find a solution. After lunch, Dave bought a hoop for about $15, pulled out a ratchet, and attached it to the backboard.

I looked at the orange rim and thought, "Wow that was easy. Why didn't I think of that?" as the first shot a kid took on the new hoop missed horribly—the child was used to shooting on a backboard without a hoop. The ball bounced hard off of the rim, but the smile on his face about being able to shoot on a real hoop made it seem like he just drained the winning shot in the NBA Finals.

This story illustrates two points that underlie the purpose of this chapter. First, sometimes it is the little things that we do as school social workers and other related-services professionals that make the biggest differences in the lives of homeless children and youth. And it is the culmination of the sometimes subtle and understated practice tasks that allow us to have a major impact. Second, homelessness can be thought of as a series of barriers and facilitators children and youth face in living their lives. This is especially important as we think about education and our practice with these youth in schools. We may be able to provide opportunities for a homeless child to attend school or get them supplies, but if they are facing such as hunger or uncertainty in their living situation, these barriers may ultimately prevent and sabotage chances for educational success. Along those lines, the barriers and facilitators we experience when we practice with homeless kids mirror the barriers and facilitators they face themselves (Canfield, 2014), meaning whatever prevents children from pursuing or obtaining educational opportunities will also hinder our practice. However, we must remember that barriers can be changed from something that prevents a sense of normalcy or equality, to something that fosters and encourages it. In the story, the playground setup went from preventing the kids playing outside to something that helped them be active.

This chapter will provide us as school social workers and related-services professionals with a practice approach that focuses on the systems that serve as either barriers or facilitators to education for homeless children. The approach outlined in this chapter should serve as a practice mindset for us working with homeless children and youth. A barrier or facilitator approach is supported by the overarching policy (the MVA) governing the educational rights for homeless youth and subsequent practice interventions and tasks used to address homelessness in our schools. This chapter will help provide insight into the client attributes and systems that will impact our evidence-based practice decisions. To help us illustrate different systems that serve as barriers or facilitators, we will go over several anecdotes developed from practice experiences with homeless children, youth, and their families. Each story provides an example of several situations that are common barriers or facilitators to both educational attainment for homeless children and youth and school social work practice with these students. The examples from these vignettes are then supported with findings and commentary from the body of knowledge on homeless children and youth. The discussion for the first two stories is of a general nature—they are overviews of our approach to homelessness. Discussion points for the final story are more specific to school-based practice with homeless children. The purpose of this chapter is not necessarily to provide practice tasks to address barriers or facilitators (we got that from the chapters on the McKinney-Vento Act), but to highlight systems at work that we as school-based practitioners should be aware of as we address homelessness, allowing us to form a practice mindset that incorporates the foundation knowledge from earlier on both child homelessness and the MVA.

What Is a Barrier or Facilitator?

Before we can delve into specific barriers and facilitators in the homeless experience, we need a basic understanding of the topic. Barriers and facilitators are a relatively common subject in the literature on school social work practice. Generally, barriers refer to anything that hinders practice, and vice versa, what does not hinder practice then facilitates it (Teasley et al., 2010). They share an inverse relationship—if an aspect of practice prevents an intervention, it is a barrier, but if the same aspect helps practice, it is a facilitator. Now this definition from Teasley et al. (2010) is referring to the barriers or facilitators that practitioners face as compared to what school-aged children experiencing homelessness face obtaining an education. Therefore we will need to make some adjustments to the definition and conceptualization of barriers and facilitators in order to make them suitable for our practice with homeless children and youth.

In our school-based practice with homeless children and youth, the barriers and facilitators that we face in practice should mirror what our homeless students face. What prevents (or helps) a child from obtaining an education should also prevent (or help) us from practicing with them (Canfield, 2014). An example would be transportation: If getting to school prevents a child from obtaining and education, then it would also prevent us from intervening with the student. For those working with homeless children and youth in school settings, barriers and facilitators are elements or systems that either prevent or aid educational opportunities (Canfield, 2014). This is particularly important because the policies that govern many of our interventions revolve around removing barriers homeless children face. We can characterize the homeless experience as a series of barriers, often due to transience, which prevent a child from obtaining an education (Jullianelle & Foscarinis, 2003), and again, the barriers and facilitators we as school-based practitioners face mirror the ones these children face (Canfield, 2014).

Thinking about Common Barriers and Facilitators

To start our discussion on barriers and facilitators to practice with homeless children, the first story will highlight some general systems at play in our practice. Oddly enough, the story is about milk, or at least children's perceptions of daily (or using a terrible pun, dairy) living activities. It is based on an experience I had working with homeless children and youth and I highlight an overarching aspect of practice that can easily be a barrier or facilitator. In addition, this story also shows that assumptions, even what seem like relatively innocuous ones, can hinder practice with the homeless.

Vignette: Milk

The children would play "Frogger," a videogame in which one tried to navigate a frog from one pond, across busy traffic, to another pond, every afternoon after school. The only problem with this was that they substituted themselves for the frog. The children were residents of a transitional housing facility and would cross a relatively busy four-lane street to get from the facility to a gas station almost every day.

The gas station was painted white, but only the top of the store reflected the original color scheme. The bottom was covered with black grime and the occasional plant growing from a crack in the wall. About every six weeks or so, there would be a sign on the station's door that said they had temporarily lost their liquor license and could not sell beer. The gas station was known for selling beer, at a healthy markup of course, to underage college kids and every now and then the police would collect a small fine and put signs in the windows. The tiles inside always felt as if there was a perpetual layer of dust or even silt that would leave these darkened brown beams on the floor when they did mop. The children would disappear into the store, purchase what they wanted, and play a second round of Frogger back to the house. There never seemed to be a problem with the kids stealing or causing trouble because the storekeeper himself never crossed the street.

The case managers at the house saw this daily game of dodging cars, and took the kids aside and gave them a safety lecture. The next day the kids walked down a block to the crosswalk, crossed the street when it was clear, and then went to the store. After a couple weeks of safer sojourns to the station, one of the case managers had concerns about what the kids were buying. As part of the transitional housing facility's programs, food (breakfast, lunch, dinner, and an after-school snack) was provided, but aside from an empty snack package here or there, he did not really see anything consistently that would ruin an appetite or at the very least be something a doting parent would disapprove. He asked the children, "What are you guys getting at the gas station? I haven't seen a lot of snack wrappers or candy or things like that."

"Milk," the children reported.

"Milk?" the case manager asked with a bewildered almost incredulous look.

"Yeah. See," they said as they showed the social worker their pints of milk, "milk."

"You don't have to go buy milk every day, we keep it here."

The children all gave him a weird look, similar to when one tries to explain to kids how Santa Claus could not possibly get to all of the houses in the world in one night. Seeing this look, he took them to the kitchen area to show them.

"See, we keep it in here," he told the kids as he pointed to the fridge.

"That's what you use it for?" one of the kids asked.

"Uh … yeah," the social worker replied, unsure if he heard that a child just asked him the purpose of a fridge. He opened the door and pulled out a gallon of milk, "see, milk. You can pour yourself a glass whenever you'd like."

The children all blurted, "That's not milk!"

"Well, yeah it's skim, but …" he started to joke. No one laughed.

The children all looked at each other. One of the kids was adamant that "Milk only comes in these." He showed the case manager his cardboard pint

"Hey, what else do you keep in there? And why is it cold?" asked one of the kids.

"Food, when we aren't eating it or haven't cooked it yet," he explained, with a hint of uncertainty in his voice.

"Oh, ours was always warm and ain't had no light like yours," one of the newer kids told the group, "we ain't never kept nothin' in it."

"Well, there is milk in here. You don't have to go buy milk when you want it. Just let one of us know and we'll make sure you get some. OK?" the case manager instructed as all of the kids nodded in unison. The next day the social worker sat in his office and watched six or seven kids cross the street to the store and come back with pints of milk in small cardboard boxes.

What We Learned

When I tell this story, most people look at me incredulously. "There's no way a kid doesn't know what a fridge is," or "c'mon, if you ever go to a grocery store you know what milk comes in," are two of the most common comments I receive. To me, it shows that we often take for granted some of the "normal" childhood experiences we expect everyone to have growing up. Many of us assume everyone knows what it is like to have a working fridge, or being able to store food for later use. This idea brings us to our first barrier or facilitator: our assumptions about experiencing homelessness as a child.

Assumptions and Our Understanding of Homelessness

Almost everything we do in social work and related-services involves assumptions. Take our ecological-systems perspective: A major assumption

---

involved in this theory is that subsystems contribute more to a system than just their presence; there are relationships, input, output, and feedback that go along with being a part of a larger system (Turner, 1996). In our thinking of homelessness, people sometimes assume that homelessness is caused by a lack of affordable housing. Although this may be a major factor to why people become and stay homeless, other reasons such as natural disasters or mental health problems may also play a part in why a given person or family experiences homelessness. However, assumptions are not necessarily always bad; for example, a key assumption in systems theory is that a change in one system means all other systems will be changed (Turner, 1996), which means if we address one system, other systems will be addressed. It is the understanding of our assumptions that allows us to properly address homelessness.

Article Spotlight: An excellent article that describes how the homeless may think differently is Van Doorn's 2010 study on the perceptions of time for those experiencing homelessness. What Van Doorn found is that those experiencing homelessness often think cyclically rather than linearly. Rather than thinking ahead, or using the ideas of "next week" or "next month," they view things in cycles. For example, people may get up at a shelter, get breakfast there, go to the library during the day, get in line at a soup kitchen for dinner, and then get in line for the shelter for the evening. This cycle is repeated daily, so the homeless may start to think only in terms of the cycle they are in. This means that long-term planning may be difficult for those experiencing homelessness. While Van Doorn focused on adults, much can be inferred about children and youth. Experiencing homelessness has a much more profound impact on younger children. We can infer that this may mean that once children and youth establish perceptions of their environment, it may be difficult for them to adjust. We need to be careful when our interventions focus on long-term planning because our students may not be able to conceptualize linear time.

Van Doorn, L. (2010). Perceptions of time and space of (formerly) homeless people. *Journal of Human Behavior in the Social Environment, 20,* 218–238.

In the previous story, the social worker assumed that the kids just needed to know that milk was in the fridge. He did not take into account that these children may not have ever had milk from a gallon jug or even a working refrigerator at any other point in their lives. His intervention of showing where milk was kept, while probably helpful, did not account for this and probably ultimately failed. Our school-based practice must keep this in mind. In addition to the overarching interventions we commonly discuss (identifying homeless kids, getting them enrolled, maintaining enrollment, etc.) we must also pay attention to what happens to the students when we get them in the door. The MVA strives to give homeless children and youth an equal educational experience and opportunity, but this may be undercut if these students have not learned how to participate in a school. Some of interventions and practice focus may need to spotlight ways to help students adjust to the school and its norms, values, and mores. Too much of a focus on just the overarching and enrollment interventions can get homeless students in the door, but it may not help children and youth experiencing homelessness obtain an education.

I am interested in why the children ignored him and crossed the street to buy milk the next day. Did they not trust him? Were they used to having food in refrigerators sporadically? Was there something else at play? Homeless children are used to disappointment in relationships (Duval & Vincent, 2009) and people saying one thing one day and another on a different day, so the children may have just assumed that what was true one day was not the next. So their reluctance to change their behavior may be more of a coping strategy rather than defiance (Douglass, 1996). This has direct implications for our school-based practice. We must be cognizant and patient with homeless school-aged children who have experienced disappointment from many adults. Resistance on the part of homeless children and families is a common barrier to our practice (Groton, Teasley, & Canfield, 2013) and much of this may stem from mistrust developed over previous relationships. In practice with this population, we may have to spend more time than usual developing rapport and establishing a trusting relationship, which could be difficult given that homeless students may move and change schools often and unexpectedly.

Along those lines, we need to remember that homelessness is a constellation of systems that impact an outcome (Rafferty, Shinn, & Weitzman, 2004), and our interventions must follow this thought. Transience and disappointment may combine to make it difficult to facilitate effective interventions Therefore our interventions must be comprehensive, taking into account what the children and youth have experienced. Ecological-systems theory can help us frame our approach with homeless children by providing a scheme to include comprehensiveness. We have to remember two key assumptions in our ecological-systems perspective as we practice with homeless children and youth. First, all of systems are interrelated (Turner, 1996). This means that changing one system will change others (Turner, 1996; Payne, 2014). Second, the whole of a situation, in this case an experience of homelessness, is greater than the sum of the parts. Whole systems are bigger than the components which comprise them (Turner, 1996). We can assume then that this means changing multiple systems could possibly have an exponential impact.

For example, tasks we often address in practice include ameliorating transportation issues for homeless children and youth, address immunization requirements for enrollment, and ensure residency requirements are waived as necessary. Each separately will have its own impact, but the sum of addressing all three areas at once will have a much greater impact then addressing each one separately. In addition, we must also focus on addressing other systems outside of the child (Fredudenberger & Torkelsen, 1984). We must also keep an eye on the systemic factors that can impact our practice and our students while we focus on the barriers or facilitators present in the child's situation. As we practice with homeless children and youth, we must remember that whatever aspects we address in our practice across micro, mezzo, and macro levels will impact all of the other systems. Our tasks should include ways to make the environment of the school better prepared, more accessible, and collaborative to help children and youth experiencing homelessness. If we address multiple systems together we can have a much larger impact. As practitioners, we cannot focus solely on one aspect of homelessness—if we only focus on making sure homeless students are able to enroll without certain documentation (a common practice task with this population), we may not be able to address transportation, for example.

To summarize, we have to understand our assumptions of our practice with homeless children and youth. Our practice should be as comprehensive as possible when working with youth experiencing homelessness (Haber & Toro, 2004). The story provides a good example of a quick intervention that only addressed one system. The intervention was able to get the kids crossing the street in a safer way, but it wasn't comprehensive enough. It did not address two other important systems at work: understanding of "normal" appliances and that food products could be kept for later. The next story will help us understand some of the issues that arise when school-aged children

School-Based Practice with Homelessness

and youth experience homelessness. It will help us move from our broad understanding of homelessness and systems to more focused knowledge about the potential attributes and systems of our clients.

This next anecdote is about my worst experience as a social worker. Actually, for this chapter the story is an amalgamation of a couple of experiences and observations. Everyone in the story, except for me, is a combination of at least two people. I did this because the anecdote deals with a very heavy situation and I wanted to make sure it stayed anonymous for the people involved. I want to be honest to what I observed and experienced, so there is some minor graphic description about violence. This is not meant to sensationalize, but I really tried to capture the dry throated/kicked in the gut feeling I had watching this unfold. I wish the story was an uncommon one, but I saw it one way or another way too often.

Vignette: Sticky, Rainy Mondays

Nothing ever goes right on a rainy Monday. The coffee machine is vacationing and, like my gas tank, the printer toner is empty. Even worse, it is the end of August. Not only is my rent due in a couple of days, but living in the South, rainy days in late August are painful. Rain offers no respite from the heat, and the giant droplets stuck to me like a million slimy slugs as I slogged into my office station at the transitional housing facility.

I was a case manager at this facility and I mainly worked with single men, each of whom had a bunk in our barracks-like setup. I had a pretty solid caseload, and by that I mean I generally liked my clients. This cycle of clients was the type a social worker dreams of working with. Many of them were taking their recovery very seriously, so that meant on Monday mornings I did not have to deal with the aftermath of testosterone mixed with alcohol. I usually got the clients that needed a drill sergeant to get into housing—one to demand why they were not saving money or one who would drive them to a job interview or AA meetings. Several of them had high-number AA chips because they couldn't get a fix or a drink in prison and attributed their sobriety to the structure in prison or jail. So I had a really good caseload of hard-working, great people who just happened to have a crack or alcohol problem. Except for one: Emmett.

Even now, the mention of Emmett makes me pantomime washing my hands. Some folks are just not good people and I feel a chill in my core when I speak or think about him. My supervisor said sometimes your soul can just feel when it is next to evil. I knew his criminal history when he got into the program, but it was not my place to judge. Never is. He was in my caseload, and at the most basic level he was still a human being and deserved my acceptance of who he was and deserved my effort to help him in whatever way I could. He was a good-looking guy, with a physique that was airbrushed from prison yard workouts. He was 45 but looked 30, and was very popular with the women in the family and women's dorm. Every month I would check his bank statement as part of his treatment plan, and almost once a week there was a $20.79 charge from Walgreens. Since he didn't have any medication he was picking up, I knew he was a busy man.

I was discharging him from the program on Tuesday, so this was his last day. He got a job in his native Atlanta and found a place to stay. Outside of his 36 per pack prophylactic purchase of $20.79 from the drugstore, he was pretty frugal and saved up enough to get his own place. I was notating this in my case files when I heard a familiar shuffle and knock at my door. It was Andy, the case manager for the family dorm, and he looked flustered. The family dorm housed about eight families in an apartment-like setting. He was usually a paragon of patience and calm, so I knew the unhinged look he wore meant something big happened—or was going to happen.

"I need you to talk to Christy," he rasped in a whisper normally reserved for funerals, "today, please."

I looked at him as if he was explaining general relativity to me. I didn't really deal with the parents in the family dorm and he never "demanded" I speak to someone. When I was in the family dorm I usually just hung out with the children and taught them about dairy products.

"She told me she is leaving the program ... with Emmett."

My eyes grew to the size of two tombstones. We immediately left my office to go to his. The 30-yard walk in the mucky, muggy late August southern mist slowed us down to a funeral dirge.

Christy was waiting in Andy's office for us. She was about 28 or 30, but looked like she was in her late forties. Life had beaten her hard and the wrinkles on her face were scars from her pack-a-day smoking habit. She had two kids, each a half-sister to the other. They were two years different, but only one grade apart. The six-year old was often reading to her eight-year old sister the Berenstein Bears books we kept around. They sat in the corner of the office. The youngest one was patiently coloring a beautiful montage of three bears eating just-right porridge. The oldest one was told to sit down by Christy, but she squirmed like an unprepared undergraduate social work student taking a statistics test. Every minute or

School-Based Practice with Homelessness

so she got up to do something, and Christy would keep reminding her to sit down.

Christy did not have a substance abuse problem (outside of cigarettes) or severe mental illness, but she had two major issues in her life. First, she had a common problem many impoverished people have: she was exploited. She had this mindset that she just needed a job and that her salvation from poverty would come through working. So Christy worked very hard, almost 60 hours a week every week, but at three different places. Each place, PartitionMart, Ground Beef Royalty, and English Fuel, was very careful to never give her more than 20 or so hours a week. That meant she didn't get any benefits from any of her jobs. She also was so grateful to have a job that she would accept whatever they paid. To put this in perspective, she had to work at least two hours at any of her jobs to afford a big-size combo number 1 at Ground Beef Royalty.

However, the problem that often sentenced her to squalor was with men. From her father and now to Emmett, almost every man in her life had left a path of carnal and physical carnage.

I asked her, "So Andy tells me you are going to Atlanta with Emmett." She nodded and I continued, "Has he ever told you about why he was in prison?"

"Yes, he let his temper get the best of him and . . ."

I got really blunt as I cut her off, "This is public record that anyone can look up free. Let me tell you why he was in prison." This was an ethical gray area; it was public record and she could look it up herself online, but more importantly I would not be able to sleep if I did not do this. "He did four years in prison for beating his girlfriend so bad she was in a coma. Emmett was sentenced to four years in prison for this. Now look, prison sentences here work that for every day you have good behavior, you get like two days off your sentence that you have to serve overall."

"I know, my ex went to prison." It was for breaking Christy's jaw.

"OK, then you know what it means when I say he did every single day of his sentence then."

"Oh James, he told me how much you've been helping him with his temper. He wouldn't do that ever. Plus have you seen him around the girls? He is so good with them."

The rain had turned to a thunderstorm outside and the bushes loudly battered the window of the office. Shadows of the trees began to stalk and creep around us. I wasn't getting through so I had to switch tactics.

"Look, if you leave here, we are going to fill you and your girls' room. You were on the waiting list; you know how long it can be. If you leave, we will fill your spot that day. We can't guarantee you that we will have a spot for you and your girls when you come back."

"Look, James, Andy, I been around a lot of scumbags in my life. I think I would know one when I meet one," she giggled. Andy and I looked at each other with the same expression I think pilots use when they know their plane is going to crash.

The day after a thunderstorm during southern Augusts is actually worse. The cement acts as brimstone, giving the whole world a humid mud and dead worm stench. And everything feels as if it was transported to a sauna. I discharged Emmett from the program at 8:45a.m. as Andy did the same for Christy. The two of them, plus the girls, got on the city bus that would take them to the Greyhound bus station for their trip to Atlanta.

Andy was not feeling well, so at 9:30 he asked me if I would call the next family and do their intake, he was going home. This was always my favorite part of my job—I got to see the hope each person wore in their smiles as their problems filled with helium and lifted away from their shoulders, if no longer than for a day as we got them into the program. I saw that the next family on the list was staying at the emergency shelter about two miles away. I called the shelter and fortuitously was able to make contact with them. This was actually my favorite part of the job and I enjoyed doing intakes for any of the dorms.

"Alright Mr. Walker, we have a spot for you, your wife, and two kids. Are you still interested in coming to the program?" I asked him over the phone.

"Yes sir! When can we move in!?!?"

"Today, anytime. I'll be here until five, but I'll leave a note in case you come in later. If we have to, we can do the intensive paperwork tomorrow."

"OK, thank you so much! Thank you! I'll see you today."

Thirty-five minutes later I got a call from the secretary informing me that there was a Walker family waiting to see me. I guessed that they got lucky with the bus or took a cab, but when I got to the front office they were standing in bathtubs of sweat. Mr. Walker's shirt was almost translucent and Mrs. Walker was sitting down in one of the waiting room chairs. She had grabbed something to fan herself from the coffee table and started swinging a Runner's World magazine back and forth.

"We didn't want to take no chances so we ran here."

I smiled. I knew I would like the Walkers—they had grabbed their children and had held them as they ran the two miles from the shelter to our facility. They did not want to take any chances at all that the bed would go away.

School-Based Practice with Homelessness

A couple Mondays later, another suffocating rainy day, I was in the family dorm giving Mr. Walker his "proof of homelessness" waiver. His wife had started taking Certified Nursing Assistant training at the local community college almost immediately after coming to the program. She was able to do this through a program that let homeless people go to school for free. During a break in one of her classes, she grabbed a masonry flier for her husband. Once he had the proof that he was homeless (it was a form I had to sign) he would be eligible to go to vocational school for free and eventually become a mason.

On the way to drop off the form, I passed by Andy's office. His door was open and someone sat in the chair across from him. I heard Andy say, "Maybe James can help. Hey James, can you come in for a minute?"

I walked into the room and asked, "What can I do for y'all?"

"Well Christy is back looking for ..."

When I heard "Christy" I dropped all my papers and I did not hear the rest of what Andy was telling me. I did not recognize the woman who sat in front of me. Her left eye was swollen shut and looked like the deep burgundy crushed velvet used in casket lining. She had tried to use concealor, but could not get to every part of her massive bruise—I guessed it had to hurt too much to put the applicator in some spots. I could see the outline of four fingers on her neck, each a reddish-blue noose-like oval. Her right arm was in a sling made from an old t-shirt. Andy tried to give her a coffee, but she told us it hurt to drink. Two of her teeth had been guillotined in half by a fist, exposing the nerve causing her noticeable pain every time she drank, breathed, and spoke.

The only word I heard Andy say after Christy was Emmett. He did this over the weekend and she spent her last dollar coming back to town. She wanted to know if there was any space for her. There wasn't. The only thing I could do for her was to give her a couple bus passes to get to the battered victim shelter and get her and the kids some food. She tried to cry, but I could see her tear ducts were sandboxes. Her youngest daughter sat in the corner coloring and her oldest daughter was rearranging of all of Andy's books, both looking almost oblivious to the situation. When Christy was finally able to press the burden of the situation off of her one functioning shoulder long enough for her to stand up, she thanked us and descended into the world with her two girls following. No money, no shelter, no jobs, no hope.

What We Learned
This story is not a "fun" one to tell, and what is worse, we all have or will have these anecdotes as we practice. Christy is a combination of three women and

I hope I gave enough respect to each of them. Emmett was a combination of two men, one I worked with and one who was in someone else's caseload.

This book is about school-based practice with homeless children, but this story doesn't take place in a school or include the children very much. In fact, the children are really ancillary characters in this story—I could have told the story without including the children. I did this intentionally to highlight two considerations to our practice in schools with homeless children and youth. First, homelessness does not occur *in* schools. We cannot really address homelessness in schools; even though it is an issue that impacts what happens in schools, it is an issue that takes place outside of the boundaries of schools. We have to understand that there may be barriers or facilitators outside the scope of our practice boundaries. Second, homelessness is a traumatic experience. Children and youth who experience homelessness are often regular witnesses to violence and aggression and this can cause major problems when these students enter the school.

Sometimes we forget that children and youth only spend around 20% of their waking hours a year in school (Berliner, 2009). This means the other 80% of their lives are spent with their family, friends, and in their neighborhoods, each of which has an impact on what occurs when they come to school. Nonschool factors can play a large role in education, but they are more likely to be barriers, as opposed to facilitators, for impoverished children and youth (Berliner, 2009). In our practice with homeless school-aged youth, we should think of these nonschool factors as "general" homeless barriers or facilitators (Canfield, 2014). These are barriers or facilitators that are inherent to experiencing homelessness and are also outside the purview of the school. All of this means that there are aspects to the experience of homeless that will impact our practice, but fall outside the scope of our efforts as school social workers. For example, the domestic violence Christy's children witnessed would be a factor that occurs outside of the schools. Even though we may not be able to directly address them, they are still aspects that will have an impact on the systems we do address in school social work practice.

One of the major general homeless barriers or facilitators that we will address in practice is the family themselves. Families play a large role in our efforts to provide equal educational opportunity. As we saw in previous chapters, the policy and subsequent practice approach to addressing problems associated with homelessness defer to the parents. In terms of barriers and facilitators, the dynamics of a homeless family and the reasons they became homeless play an important role in facilitating school social work practice

(Swick, 2003). Different familial systems, such as family structure and other characteristics, will either impede or help our practice outcomes (Danesco & Holden, 1998).

Now let's examine the story and identify some of the family dynamics at play. Again, this story unfortunately is a common one for many homeless families, and the dynamics of the family would play a large role in our interventions if we were school social workers practicing with Christy's daughters. Christy worked 60 hours a week, meaning that her time may not allow her to be as involved in making decisions or participating in interventions. Next, her pay may not allow her to miss much work. (This is another great example of how two systems together make up a larger effect than their sum—she works too much, but she also cannot afford to miss work. The two have a synergistic effect.) Now the big one: The two girls have probably grown up witnessing many acts of violence against their mother. The story actually mentions three people specifically (Christy's father, her ex, and Emmett) who have perpetrated some sort of violence against Christy.

Violence is often a major factor to why single female-headed households become homeless (Anooshian, 2005; Chambers et al. 2013; Gully, Koller, & Ainsworth, 2001) and is a relatively common topic in the literature on homeless families. Findings consistently indicate that homeless children consistently experience or witness violence (Anooshian, 2005; Chambers et al. 2013; Gully, Koller, & Ainsworth, 2001), often at higher rates than their peers. All of the experiences of violence homeless children and youth experience creates a very stressful home and family life (Baggerly, 2003). Daily survival is not only a major aspect of homelessness, but a constant focus. Living without housing is a major stressor for homeless families (Banyard, 1995), and the stress from this experience in their home life leads to higher rates of mental health problems (Baggerly, 2003). Furthermore, experiences of violence can limit a homeless woman's support system and leave her with fewer resources than her peers (Bassuk et al., 1996), which makes it more difficult to leave experiences of homelessness.

Like several other barriers or facilitators, violence can be seen as occurring both in and outside of school. For our practice with children experiencing homelessness, issues such as school bullying or fighting can be a common way violence is brought into the school arena. These are areas we can address directly as school-based practitioners, and there are many resources available to help our practices with those issues (David Dupper's book, *School Bullying*, in the SSWAA series is an excellent resource). However, the effects of violent home life can still be seen in our students while they are at school. Even though we may not be able to address domestic violence directly in our schools, we can address an important byproduct: social isolation.

The idea of social isolation as a result of experiencing or witnessing abuse is one of the ways a general homeless barrier or facilitator can be observed in our school-based practice. Social isolation is not just physical distance or separation from peers (Anooshian, 2003; Kennedy, 2007), it is really a mindset. It is the lack of good interaction with peers and the absence of any attachment to society. Social isolation has been shown to increase risk of experiencing homelessness as an adult (Anooshian, 2003) and can exacerbate or lead to mental health and behavioral problems. Along these lines, homeless children often have many experiences of social rejection. Whether by peers or violence at home, social rejection leads homeless children and youth to often internalize their problems, which makes it difficult to create social support networks (Anooshian, 2003). Furthermore, the preference to be alone in social settings will have a direct impact on our practice because schools are social settings. Academic success is due in part to a child's ability to participate and navigate social situations (Anooshian, 2003).

I never paid attention to it in the moment, but how Christy's daughters acted in the office when the tension was palpable and the chaos was at the highest level was astonishing. They seemed unfazed by the entire situation. I remember as a young child being scared when I saw my Mom with a bandage on her hand from cutting herself making dinner. It is not a pleasant experience to see your parent vulnerable, but here were two girls with a mom that was beaten unrecognizable reading and sorting books. If we translate this to the playground, those girls may not display the appropriate reactions to common cues, further isolating them from their peers. They found ways, though probably unhealthy, to cope among the chaos. The next anecdote will explore experiencing homelessness from a student's perspective.

Vignette: Ice Cream and Hoodies Background

The following vignette is more specific to practice with homeless children and youth. Essentially, it is the story of a day in the life of a teen experiencing homelessness. It is written from the youth's perspective and is based off of several teens I have worked with through practice and volunteer work, but mainly in several research studies I have conducted. Many of their comments made their way directly into the story. In addition, I also drew from the work of Dr. Dana Harley, whose innovative and nationally recognized work about hope and barriers to graduation with homeless and at-risk youth led to much insight on the day-to-day life of homeless youth. Her work provides a direct avenue into the lexicon of teens and how they perceive the world. One particular part of the story is directly inspired by Rick Remender's excellent comic book *Deadly Class*; issues one and three are definitely worth a read if you are interested in child homelessness.

As a note, I wrote this in the vernacular of the children and youth who inspired the story. In a small way I wanted to try and give them a voice. One of the things you learn researching or working with this population is that many feel that they do not get heard in their lives. So I did my best to write this how it has been told to me. But in doing so, some of the grammar may be a little "rough." There is some slang used, but hopefully much of it is described. Again, this anecdote is based on the stories told to me when I listen to the homeless children and youth I work with.

Vignette: Ice Cream and Hoodies (Part One)

I don't need no alarm. Dudes be coming by trying to gank yo' stuff before we all gotta get up. I ain't gettin' my shoes ganked. Nuh uh. I need them. My momma ain't got no car so I gotta walk everywhere. Good pair of "J's" take me everywhere.

Hack! Hack!

I hate coughs. They hurt. I can't breathe too good right now. Every time I cough it hurt. Boogers be comin' up and it hurt. It's all good—at least I ain't got no headache no more.

Dude that run this place gettin' ready to turn on the light. It be 5 in the morning. We all gotta get out by 5:30. It suck because my momma and sister stay in the other room. They ain't gotta get out til 6. They got locked in that room. If you a boy, you gotta be under 13 to stay in the room with yo' momma. If you a girl you gets to stay in there. Don't matter yo' age.

I ain't gotta stay with my momma for like three years now. It's my birthday, so that means I get to have ice cream today. The DQ be giving out free ice cream on yo' birthday so you know I gotta get there. That ice cream gonna be good. I'm gonna share it with my sister. She cool. She like six but she tough.

Dude next to me pissed hisself. I hate when they do that. Last week dude pissed hisself so bad it soaked my mat too. He ain't piss hisself so bad today. I gotta get to the bathroom before anybody get to doodoo in it. It be stank in there and ain't nobody know how to flush if I ain't there first. I gotta brush my teeth. I ain't changing my clothes today, but I always got clean teeth. That means I take care of myself.

Hack! Hack! Hack!

I hate this damn cough. Ice cream gonna feel real good.

Hack! Hack! Hack!

I ain't changing today so I just be dipping out real quick. I ain't dealing with no foolishness today. Cop always be looking at me when I leave. He always tellin' me go to school and keep my grades up. He tellin' me that today. "Make sure you get yourself to school today young man, that is how you stay out of places like this." Man, like I got a choice. My momma left her boyfriend cause he an ass, so we all gotta leave. That be why I staying here again. Been two weeks. Every time my momma leave her dude we gotta come back, but we ain't been here since summer. One time we stay at a church for a month, but they ain't want us there no more.

I ain't want to deal with nothing when they make piss-guy get up. Dudes that drink go ape-wild when you wake 'em in the morning. I gotta spot outside the McDonalds where they ain't hassle me so I can wait for my momma and sister. One time this lady that work there give me a sandwich and orange juice. She ain't even charge me. She don't work there no more.

Hack! Hack! Hack!

All dudes be leavin' so that means the 33 bus and 45 bus gotta go by and then my momma and sister come out. The 45 bus gonna take me to DQ and back so it be easy for me and my sister later today. I usually walk, that's why I don't want my "J's" ganked, but I got two bucks. That's enough to pay for my sister and me to take the bus. We walk back.

Hack! Hack! Hack!

I hate the boogers that be coming up.

Hack! Hack! Hack!

My momma and sister be out. I gotta take my sister to her bus stop first. My momma don't say nothing to me when she give me Triana. Momma gotta work a double at PartitionMart. She don't like working no doubles. Triana go to school later than me, but she get picked up first. Where we used to be stayin' at, she get picked up last and I be first. Whatever. She be tough. She ain't allowed to go to school last week cause she beat some girl trying to gank her tater tots.

That's why I don't get why that cop dude always be telling me to go to school. At school I get to eat guaranteed. I go buck-wild too if someone gank my tater tots.

Hack! Hack!

Ice cream gonna be good.

Hack!

My sister and I walk to her bus stop. Everybody knows my sister be tough. They ain't say a word to her. Bus come and they get on.

Hack! Hack! Hack! COUGH! Hack!

This be hurtin' but I still got to go to school, I'm gonna smash—lunch gonna be good!

Hack!

I hate this man, I hate this part. They put my stop at 7th and MLK. The Haven is at 5th and MLK. You can see it when I get on the bus. All them people know who get picked up at this stop. But whatever. Today my birthday, so I get ice cream.

I the only one at this stop today. Sometime they be other kids, but I be the only one today. I can see the bus come which be good. It chilly and gonna be rainy. I glad I got two dollars so I can take my sister and I to DQ on the city bus. We can walk back but we gonna have ice cream so it ok.

Hack! Hack! Hack!

There be three stops before we get to school so bus be mostly full. I hate this. I hate this. I hate this. I done gave myself a headache I hate this. My momma say don't fight. When Triana got in that fight cause she ain't want that girl ganking her tater tots, my momma say she got to go to the school to talk. That mean she gotta leave work. Her boyfriend didn't like that. Plus last week she gotta watch Triana so she ain't go to work. At least they ain't fire her. Her boss cool.

Hack! Hack!

I hate this. When I get on the bus I wanna find a seat by myself. You got to ask to sit down if someone else already in the seat. Last week I gotta ask a white girl if I can sit down and she was all like "eeeewwww, you smell like pee" cause piss-guy piss too much and it got on my mat.

Hack! Hack! Hack!

I hate this but there be an empty seat. Thank God. Its my birthday. I can hear that white girl go like "why is he wearing that? Didn't he wear that yesterday? And all like last week? O.M.G.? What a loser? Doesn't he pay attention?" it sound like all her sentences be questions. Whatever. We going to Luthor High School but I got a Kent High hoodie on. They colors be red and blue, but Luthor be green and black. Kent be giving out hoodies to everyone on the first day. That's where I was first day. But now it like February. I been going here a week. Last week was my first week at Luthor. Week before that I ain't go, week before that I be at Kent. I was there twice. I started there, then when we staying at that church I be going to Lane, then my momma got back with her boyfriend when the church ain't want us no more, so I go back to Kent. Now I at Luthor. Luthor ain't give no sweatshirt on first day so I be happy that I was at Kent to start. My momma gotta pay like $150 to get me in Luthor. They say her address mean I supposed to be in Kent, but I could transfer if we pay $150. Summertime don't matter cause I ain't got to go to school.

Hack! Hack! Hack!

I hate this. I can hear white girl point at me to her friends. They think it funny that I be wearing a Kent shirt that I wore yesterday. Whatever. They was like, "Do you know where he sleeps? Like O.M.G. tragic?" They acting like I can't hear them. Whatever. I hate this. But I'm getting ice cream.

Barriers in Part One
Transience

One of the first barrier we should examine is transience. The idea of transience is a major focus of homeless literature in general (McAllister et al., 2010, Sosin, 2003). This topic is a major aspect of how we conceptualize homelessness. Oftentimes we call homelessness an experience of transience, and for we who are practicing in schools, the byproduct of transience is school mobility. In the story, the main character mentions that in the past school year he has attended three different schools, with a possible fourth on the horizon. This high amount of school mobility can cause major problems and disruptions to his pursuit of education.

Moving between schools can be a very difficult experience in general. However, it's the unplanned nature of homeless children moving between schools that is much more detrimental to academic achievement (Weckstein, 2003). Very rarely do families prepare to be homeless—many of the causes of homelessness are related to trauma (fleeing domestic violence, natural disaster, etc.) or are a result of poverty and being precariously housed, not necessarily out of planned choice. If we think about this from the child's perspective, unplanned school mobility can be very traumatic. They may not get an opportunity to say goodbye to friends at their old school. They will have to get used to a new schedule, the nuances of new teachers, and a new routine. In our story, the main character makes mention of the fact that there is a new bus schedule. While he stays at the shelter, his sister gets picked up earlier whereas he used to get picked up first at his old school.

As it relates to school and education, homeless children experiencing these unplanned school interruptions and unplanned school mobility often score lower on standardized tests, have poor academic outcomes, and are at high risk for dropout (Alexander, Entwisle, & Horsey, 1997; Urban Institute, 2010; Julianelle & Foscarinis, 2003). A unique way that unplanned school mobility can cause additional problems is that many extracurricular activities, such as sports teams or drama productions, require students to attend school for a certain amount of time, or have attendance restrictions. Being unable to participate in school activities that other students are eligible for may make it difficult to make friends and develop a social network, leading to emotional, mental, and social problems as well (Julianelle & Foscarinis, 2003). Hamann, Mooney, and Vrooman's (2002) report on standards for programs that serve homeless children and indicate that increasing stability, thus reducing transience, is necessary for quality interventions.

Attendance

Many of our interventions with homeless school-aged youth involve improving attendance problems (Jullianelle & Foscarinis, 2003). Theoretically, if a homeless child is regularly attending school, some semblance of stability is obtained. Because of this, addressing attendance issues are a major concern for those practicing with this population. In the case example, the student still attended school, though he spoke of missing a week because he was in between housing locations. Oftentimes, homeless school children are at high risk for missing an inordinate amount of school days (Miller, 2009a; Rafferty et al., 2003). We attribute the high rate of poor attendance back to transience and unplanned school mobility (Dworak-Fisher, 2009; Jozefowicz-Simbeni & Israel, 2006; Jullianelle & Foscarinis, 2003) because there is often disconnect between leaving one school and enrolling in another.

Attendance is important for us to think about because it is one of the few areas that we as school social workers and other related-services personnel can directly address. In the story about Christy, school-based practitioners may not be able to directly address domestic violence, but we can use our resources to provide options to her children to help get her girls in school. Second, poor attendance is almost always linked with negative academic outcomes (Roby, 2004). Higher attendance leads to higher reading, writing, and math scores (Roby, 2004) and it is especially crucial to younger students because that is the time when foundation skills and knowledge are taught. If children miss the foundations of learning, they are at much higher risk for dropout and other negative academic outcomes. Finally, if a child consistently misses school, the ability to diagnose and address possible learning disabilities is severely hampered (Jozefowicz-Simbeni & Israel, 2006). For homeless children who move unexpectedly, the process to diagnose and treat a learning disability often starts over when they change schools, further placing children and youth experiencing homelessness behind their peers. To prevent this, it is necessary for a continuance of care and services as a child moves between schools.

Vignette: Ice Cream and Hoodies (Part Two)

Hack! Hack! Hack!

First period be math class. I'm real good at this math class. I already took this class last year when I was at Olsen so I know all the answers. Plus I sit in the back corner. Ain't nobody see me cause I get to class first. Second period suck. It be English. I ain't got no problem, but Mrs. Metallo be trippin'—she be telling us we gotta turn in our paper on the computer. She yell at me cause I turned in my assignment on notebook paper. Whatever, I got good shoes so I can walk to the library. She ain't bad, she just old. I ain't care. I been here one week and she already gave me a book. Why I got read a book about someone name Oliver in England? I don't live there.

Hack! Hack! Hack!

Third period be biology. We gotta cut up a worm today. I be lucky in this class. White girl I sit next to don't like cutting stuff. Then why she take biology? Last year at Olsen I did this one too. So she do the paperwork, I do the cutting. I be good at it. I know that you gotta be careful at the butt when you cutting a worm. You go too deep you be turning everything black because worm doodoo look like dirt. Plus this white girl be like the only one that be telling me she like my hoodie. She do the paperwork so we a good team. This class always go by quick when we gotta cut stuff. I do the worm, she do the paper.

I get in trouble a lot in fourth period. I just be getting sleepy. Mr. Wayne ain't a bad guy, it just he kinda always serious. I done did the math. I been up seven and a half hours now. Plus history be boring. This people in charge. This people fight them. Then they in charge. Then we go to the next. My eyes be closing.

I don't remember nothin' but I guess Mr. Wayne see me sleeping. He staring right at me standing in front of my desk. He say he want to talk to me after class. Why so serious? Whatever. I try to stay awake, but he keep talking about how people be in charge and now they ain't.

Hack! Hack! Hack!

I gotta talk to Mr. Wayne. That be OK. I don't like fifth period anyway. It be economics. So it be good cause I know Mr. Wayne gonna yell at me and it gonna take me into fifth period so I be allowed to be late.

Hack! Hack! Hack!

He be sitting at his desk and then he askin' why I'm sleeping. I tell him I don't know. He ask if I get enough sleep. I shake my head up and down. I be lying, but he ain't gonna find out. Now I know it gonna be coming from him, he be telling me how I slept everyday last week and now today. I just stand there, it be over soon. I just want the detention. I'm going to the bathroom when he done before I go to econ. I ain't gotta go, but that mean I get out a little more econ.

Hack! Hack! Hack!

Why is he asking me if I know Mrs. Byars? Is she the principal? Cause now I got to go see her. But now I ain't gotta go to econ. That's cool—I'll trade econ for lecturin' any day.

Hack! Hack! Hack!

Mr. Wayne be walking me down personally. First he called, then now he walking me down. I guess Luthor really don't like sleeping. Whatever. It beat econ.

Hack! Hack! Hack!

We walking to the office, but we ain't go to the principal office. I ain't be at Luthor long so I don't know if sleeping be illegal here. I only been to the office on first day, when principal be lecturing, and when I gotta see the truant cop. Today ain't first day and we done passed the principal office.

Hack! Hack! Hack!

Mrs. Byars office be lame. All school people be having the same designer. They always be some poster of a mountain saying "determination" or something stupid. Like a mountain can determine nothing. Whatever. At least she got one of them bunny coffee mugs. It be saying "I ain't spoiled, I deserve all this." She one that likes to pretend to clown I bet, but I bet she serious, but not like Mr. Wayne. Ain't nobody that serious.

Hack! Hack! Hack!

Mrs. Byars be a white lady too. She dressed like we be at church. She always smiling. She tell me she a social worker, but she trippin' cause social workers only be talking to my momma about her dude beating on Triana.

That's why Triana tough. She telling me Mr. Wayne be saying I'm sleeping a lot and she worried. Whatever. She ain't worried about me—she worried about her job. Now she telling me some of the other teachers notice I always be wearing the same jeans and Kent hoodie. Why everybody here care what I wearing? She trying to joke about how that be "Crip-toe-night" here, but I don't know why that be funny—I don't mess around with gangs, Crips or Bloods. She see that I ain't laughing so she change the subject. Cough. Cough. I don't wanna cough too loud in her office. Her coffee mug be too close to me.

She ask me where I be crashin' at night and I tell her the Haven and then she look my file up. She say she sorry cause she shoulda pick up on that sooner cause my momma put the Haven address as our home. Mrs. Byars now talking about something about policy and stuff. I hope I ain't in trouble. She ask me if I wanna wash my clothes. Why she asking me that? I wanna cause momma ain't give me no quarters for the Laundromat in a while. I tell her I ain't got nothing else to wear. She say that OK she got stuff. She be telling me the athletics got a washer and dryer so it be ok to wash my clothes whenever as long as I go with her. I ask her how much. She look at me funny and say it be free. She don't seem that bad. She walk me down to the gym but we don't stop at the basketball court. We keep walking.

Hack!

Now we back by the equipment room. Mr. Wayne be there too. He coach of the wrestling team.

Hack! Hack! Hack! I hate this damn cough, but ice cream gonna be good.

Dang! They givin' me an Under Armour hoodie! Mr. Wayne said that Mrs. Byars say I be needing it. He also giving me Under Armour shorts. He say don't call em basketball shorts cause they say KHS wrestling. Then he say something like ain't no wrestling things got nothing to do with basketball. He can tell me those shorts be called whatever cause they nice. He say they leftover from last year and ain't nobody pick them up so I can have them free. Dang! I like Mrs. Byars, she make things happen.

Hack! Hack! Hack!

Now Mrs. Byars say we got to go back up to her office. She say Mr. Wayne is doing wrestling laundry now anyway so my clothes be OK. She say she want to talk to me more tomorrow. I ask her if we can do it during fifth period cause I ain't like econ. She say no, we gotta do it in fourth. That's OK, it just be about people in charge that ain't alive no more. She gives me a note to give to Mrs. Saad because I miss almost all of econ. God be loving me today.

Hack! Hack!

Mrs. Byars don't like that last cough. She tell me hold up cause she getting the nurse. The nurse tell me come to her office. She make me lift my Under Armour hoodie and put that thingy that makes her hear better on me and tell me to breathe. She be shaking her head cause she like it sound real bad and I need an x-ray of my chest. She write me up a note and say that I need to go to the clinic. She trippin' cause the clinic be four miles away. I got good shoes but I ain't got that good shoes. Ain't nobody remember that you gotta walk back, that mean it really eight miles.

Mrs. Byars tell me I gotta go to class now but tomorrow during fourth period she gonna talk to me. We gonna go over a couple different things. She saying we gonna get help together. She be getting me stuff so I be cool with it. Plus when I was leaving the door she told me happy birthday.

Hack!

Lunch be cool. We ain't gotta fill out no paperwork to get free lunch here. Everybody eat for free. That also mean people ain't trying to gank my fries. Some people gank fries cause they jerks, but I know I ganked fries cause I was hungry so I don't get too mad when other people be doing it unless I be hungry too. I know it look like it about to rain, but I be sitting outside today. I like this big tree they got outside. It be huge. It make me feel good cause all this buildings be around it but it still be here. It ain't get cut down. If it can be here, I can too.

Hack! Hack! Hack!

This be hurting. I gonna go talk to Mrs. Byars tomorrow. She make things happen, so maybe I can get a buncha cough drops.

Hack!

Sixth period be Spanish and it boring, but we watching a video today. I can close my eyes.

I open them when the bell ring. Now I got to go to gym. I already dressed cause I got basketba—I mean wresting shorts on. Gym teacher tells me that its nice that I dressed out for once. We be weightlifting today so it be easy. I like weightlifting. Plus gym at the end of the day mean I get to the bus quicker cause the locker room be next to the buses.

Barriers in Part Two
Obtaining Records

Smooth transitions between schools are needed for positive educational outcomes (Jullianelle & Foscarinis, 2003). A very subtle part of the story was when the student mentioned that he had taken the math class before. This indicates that he may have been placed into the wrong course upon enrollment in his new school. We can speculate that this was the school's best attempt to place the child in the right classes given that the parents either did not bring, or authorize the school to obtain, the appropriate records. If the school knew that the child was homeless, then this is the right approach, at least according to policy. We want to get homeless children into school immediately, and then we can adjust from there. However, homeless students may have many unmet needs in regard to special education and placement into these programs is crucial for addressing these needs (Zima & Forness, 1997). The longer we wait before correctly placing children in the appropriate classes, the poorer the outcomes (Zima & Forness, 1997). Therefore our ability to get the appropriate records for homeless children and youth can be an important aspect to our practice and can truly help facilitate services.

Communication

The next barrier or facilitator we should discuss is communication. Dworak-Fisher (2009) contends that schools must communicate with homeless families by providing information on the rights to education for their children. Not only is this part of federal policy, but it is also necessary to communicate with homeless families to ensure that we are able to provide the services needed for educational attainment. Studies have indicated that awareness of educational rights for homeless children remains low (Zima, Wells, & Freeman, 1994) and even if families are aware, they may lack the necessary resources to achieve goals (Yousey, Leake, Wdowik, & Janken, 2007). So for single female-headed households in which violence may be an issue, as in this story and Christy's, awareness of rights may still pose a problem if social capital and resources are low.

In our story, it was clear that the mother and child did not know about the services available or their educational rights. Homeless children have the right to stay in the same school even if their housing situation takes them out of the district's residential boundaries, but the main character reported that he had attended several different schools over the course of the year. How well we communicate with homeless families may play a large role in being able to identify our clients and provide the services needed to help children obtain educational opportunities.

Identification

In order to practice, we need clients. If clients are unavailable to be served, then practice cannot occur. Because homeless school children move unexpectedly between schools, maximizing the time a child may be enrolled in a given service area is important (Jozefowicz-Simbeni & Israel, 2006). Furthermore, in order to address the needs of homeless children, one must know whether a child is experiencing homelessness (Dworak-Fisher, 2009; Glassman et al., 2010; Herrington et al., 2006). Several factors, such as embarrassment or resistance, prevent homeless children from requesting services (Jullianelle & Foscarinis, 2003), and identifying homeless children in schools remains one of our most difficult challenges as practitioners (Dworak-Fisher, 2009; Glassman, Karno, & Erdem, 2010; Herrington, Kidd-Herrington, Kritsonis, 2006). Services hinge on the proper identification of homeless children and, without identification, services cannot be provided.

We must actively search for homeless children within our service area (Dworak-Fisher, 2009), and federal policies require that districts employ a liaison to reach out to the homeless population (Dworak-Fisher, 2009; Herrington et al., 2006). These liaisons must also inform homeless families of the policies and provisions available (Jozefowicz-Simbeni & Israel, 2006). Identification of homeless children is often mentioned in the literature but unfortunately has not been empirically studied. The use or effectiveness of liaisons in identifying homeless children is an avenue that deserves greater attention and should garner more research. Because the topic of identification plays such an important role in the providing of homeless services, we need to develop a better understanding of how we can improve our efforts identifying homeless children and youth.

Anecdotally, I have heard of many different ways homeless children have been identified. In one instance a janitor found a child sleeping in a bathroom stall after school hours. Another story I heard from a practitioner was that a lunch lady continually caught a child stealing food, but not candy or snacks like most kids. The child was getting the standard cafeteria meal and then just walking out of the serving area without paying. Unfortunately, the common description of homeless families and children as the invisible poor or an invisible problem rings true in our practice as we try to identify homeless children and youth for services. We must be careful to avoid stereotypes in our thoughts on homeless children and youth. For example, in my first study analyzing school data to assess the impact of homelessness on academic outcomes, the research team was surprised to find that several of the students identified as homeless were honor roll students enrolled in advanced placement courses. This challenged

---

our assumption that homeless children are a homogenous group, but reinforced the idea that homelessness is an experience that impacts each child differently.

As stated earlier, there are not many studies that provide empirical scientific evidence about what can improve identification of homeless students. However, through speaking with many homeless liaisons and helping schools address homelessness, I feel that collaboration is a key component to successful identification. In the story, there are three points at which identification could have been made. First, upon enrollment, the mother used the address of the shelter. I've seen and heard of numerous situations in which the person in charge of enrollment noticed the home address was that of a shelter or that the shelter address had been flagged for referral to a liaison. Second, the bus driver may have been able to provide valuable information about who got picked up and where. Most likely the bus driver knew what the student knew: Whoever was picked up at this particular spot was most likely staying at the shelter. I've seen firsthand that a child was identified for services because the bus driver happened to tell the liaison over a friendly lunch that she was picking up a child at an unofficial stop (this was a little more common in a rural areas, especially when everyone sort of knows everyone), because the mother's housing situation changed and her family was sleeping in her sister's garage. Finally, the teacher noticed that the child was sleeping consistently in his class and had the forethought to dig deeper about the cause of the problem. With other issues such as behavioral problems or physical disabilities, the evidence for identification is easily observable. We can notice when a child is severely oppositional or may have difficulty with vision. Homelessness, however, does not necessarily leave clear and obvious clues. At times we may have to notice the subtle signs in order to properly identify children. More importantly we need to make sure all of the systems within a school, from administration to teachers to people serving lunch, are aware and willing to address homelessness (Haber & Toro, 2004; Reed-Victor & Pelco, 1999).

Vignette: Ice Cream and Hoodies (Part Three)
Hack!

I be the first on the bus so I get my own seat. That white girl look at me like why I got a Luthor sweatshirt. She ain't like that cause we wearing the same one now but hers is smaller. I smile.

I counted it, 15 coughs til my stop. I don't even care that everybody knows why I get off here, I'm bout to get ice cream! I just gotta wait for my sister. I hope she was good today. I don't want momma to miss more work.

Hack! Hack! Hack!

I hang out at the McDonalds til Triana bus be here. She get off. She tell me she was good today cause I told her if she wasn't I wasn't sharing my ice cream. I remember that now. Haha! I share it with her even if she pulled that girl hair again. She be telling me they friends now anyways so it's all good.

Hack! Hack! Hack!

She got the cough too now. We wait for the 45 city bus, but it don't take long. We the only ones getting on and ain't nobody getting off. I take out my two bucks and driver be like they raised the price it now be $1.10 each. That shouldn't be no thing, because I'm like she six! If you young you pay half fare. Bus driver be like that be for people five or younger. I ain't got no more so I grab Triana and we gonna walk. It be ok. It only like 2 miles and I got good shoes.

Hack! Hack! Hack!

It starting to rain now. Ain't hard, but it suck.

Hack! Hack! Hack!

The 45 bus pass us two more times before we get to DQ. All the way we be talking about what we want. God be smiling today. Cause now I got two dollars since we ain't get on the bus. Triana gonna get her own. She gonna get chocolate. I'm getting swirl.

Hack! Hack! Hack!

We just bout there. My throat and chest hurt, but it be OK, ice cream gonna help.

Hack!

All the lights be off at DQ. The door got a sign on it. It say "By order of the Health Department this establishment is closed." What that mean? That mean I can't get no ice cream? I try opening the door but it be locked. Piss-guy come up to me cause he hanging out by the umbrellas at the outside tables. He ain't never remember me. He tell me they closed it cause the milk ain't be stored at the proper temperature too many times.

Hack! Hack! Hack!

Triana tough so she don't cry. But I guess we ain't gettin' ice cream. My throat hurt.

Hack! Hack! Hack!

We gotta walk back, but I got an idea. I go into the garbage and find a DQ cup. It a little sticky inside but that be OK. I walk down another block, this time to 35th cause there be some shops. Two dudes be talking to each other. They be talking about the Super Bowl. One guy says "I bet you $500 bucks the Patriots will win." Other guy say "you're on cause the Giants never lose to them in the playoffs—you better pay up." "You're right. I paid up last week's bet didn't I?" I go up to them and say you got any change? And show em my cup. Then they be like "I ain't got money like that!" And push me away. All I need is twenty cent to ride the bus with me and Triana.

Now there be a fat dude walking down the street. I ask him, "Change? I just need a little to take the bus." He tell me "I know what you need young man" and hand me a paper. He tell me they got plenty of job openings in the classifieds as he walk away. I ain't need a job. It just be raining and my chest hurt. I just wanna ride the bus.

Hack! Hack! Hack!

I just gonna put Triana on the 45 bus by herself. Ain't nobody giving me change. It raining too hard for people to stop. I give her directions about what she supposed to do on the bus cause it be coming so we getting ready. It be a different driver. He be like "you both getting on?" and I'm like "No, I only got two bucks and she si . . ." and then he tell me, "Stop. She five." So we can both get on. He probably ain't gonna be a bus driver for too much longer.

We play a game to see who can cough the least on the way back. It a counting game. That type of stuff helps out little kids. I cough seven times until the McDonalds where we get off. Triana coughs eight.

We see momma and Triana run to her. Momma look happy. She say that we got a place to stay. Auntie letting us sleep in her shed for a little bit. She live in the country so it be a half hour drive, but that closer to momma's work so it better. Now momma ain't gotta take two buses.

Auntie live out by Perry High.

OH SNAP!

I forgot my clothes at Luthor. I tell my momma but she say, "tough we gotta go now." She and auntie don't like each other too much, but Auntie is here with her car to drive us. I tell momma Mrs. Byars wants to meet me tomorrow at fourth period. Momma say she don't care, we ain't staying at The Haven tonight. Momma tell me that I gotta catch the city bus on my own to get to the school bus stop if I want to go tomorrow. I ain't got no cash. She say it my fault I ain't got no clothes 'cept the ones I be wearing. She say that she work tomorrow, but she got the day off after that so she gonna get me in Perry the day after if they ain't charging nothin' for going there. If they do, we gotta wait til after pay day. Whatever.

What We Learned

The situations in this anecdote were told to me by several different homeless children and youth. Again, I wanted to try and get their story out in their own terms. There are a lot of concrete examples of the systems that are barriers or facilitators in this story. In fact, there are a lot of different practice points, areas for further examination, and highlights to make in this story, but I am only going to focus on some of the major barriers in the story. I wanted to provide a realistic story about what a homeless child experiences that was not trite, patronizing, or written in a research style. If you are able to use this story in any way to help illustrate a point or teach with it, by all means please do. This next section will focus on some of the common barriers or facilitators that were brought up in the story.

Barriers in Part Three
Embarrassment

Continuing with the idea of subtle and small systems can have major impacts in the lives of homeless youth, bus stops can be a major barrier. Or more so, the embarrassment of other students knowing a stop is for kids at a shelter can make life very difficult for homeless children and youth. In a great example of how one system impacts another, moving a bus stop one block away so that the kids staying in a shelter could be dropped off at a recreation center and park rather than in front of a shelter anecdotally reduced bullying and problems amongst the students. Julianelle and Foscarinis (2003) provide stories wherein homeless school children have academic problems associated with feelings of embarrassment. The authors contend that some homeless children do not wish to seek services for fear of being "outed," meaning their peers will find out about their situation. The small act of having the same sweatshirt as other people could go a long way to helping the child feel welcomed and a part of the school. There is little literature as to the extent embarrassment and stigma impact school social work practice, indicating this is another gap that needs to be addressed in studies.

Well-Being

It is well documented that homeless children and youth experience many problems with their well-being. Homeless children have problems associated with poor nutrition, poor mental health, and stunted physical development (Dworak-Fisher, 2009; Menke, 1998; Rafferty & Shinn, 1991; Shinn et al. 2008). Many times homeless children suffer developmentally because they are unable to explore their surroundings. For example shelter rules may prevent a child from playing freely in an environment or there may be exposed wiring or other harmful situations in an abandoned building. Asthma is a major problem for children experiencing homelessness (Cutuli, Herbers, Rinaldi, Masten, & Oberg, 2010), as is poor oral health (DiMarco, Huff, Kinion, & Kendra, 2009). As we think about well-being, it is not only what the child may suffer from but also access to services. In the story, the nurse suspected pneumonia but needed to have the child obtain a chest x-ray to be sure. The student was given a referral but did not have true access to the help he needed.

Common Barriers and Facilitators to Practice with Homeless Children and Youth

Transience/Instability

Homeless school-aged children and youth often move between housing situations and schools. This is thought to be a major factor as to why homeless children have such poor outcomes.

Identification

Many homeless children and families do not identify themselves for services. In addition, the definition of homelessness includes situations that many may not consider homeless.

Attendance

Homeless children miss an inordinate amount of school compared to their peers.

Communication

Homeless families often have low awareness of the MVA. School faculty, staff, and administration must also communicate what they observe to better help identification.

Personal Resources

Homelessness can be thought of as a period of deprivation, and homeless children and youth may not have the resources to succeed academically.

Transportation

Transportation is often cited as a major hurdle to getting homeless children in school, though having solid and collaborative plans in place to transport children to school has been shown to help attendance.

Community Resources

Homelessness occurs outside of the school. They systems available in a given community can help or hinder our practice.

Cultural Competence

We often need to understand the cultural context of our clients in general. Because minorities are overrepresented in the homeless counts, homelessness can be considered a defacto cultural competency issue.

Family

Policies that govern our practice defer to the families. We must ensure they know their rights and provide them with the resources to help their children succeed.

Embarrassment/Resistance

Many families and children do not wish to identify themselves out of embarrassment.

Policies

Policies schools create to address homelessness are major factors in our success.

School Administration

How administration views the issue of homelessness impacts how we will act about the issue.

Student Compliance

Our policy-shaped practice approach only provides for opportunity.

Obtaining Records

This can help or hinder the education of a child. If a child is placed too far ahead or behind when moving to a new school, academic delays and frustration may set in.

Physical Well-Being

Poor health is often associated with homelessness.

References: Buckner, 2008; Burt, 2003; Dworak-Fisher, 2009; James & Lopez, 2003; Jozefowicz-Simbeni & Israel, 2006; Jullianelle & Foscarinis, 2003; Larsen, 2002; McAllister, Kuang, & Lennon, 2010; Menke, 1998; Miller, 2009a; O'Leary, 2001; Rafferty & Shinn, 1991; Rafferty, Shinn, & Weitzman, 2004; Sosin, 2003; Swick, 2003; Weckstein, 2003; Wong, Salomon, Elliott, Tallarita, & Reed, 2004.

Summary

This chapter provided us with an overview of how we should approach school social work practice with homeless children and youth. We need to focus on the systems that serve as barriers or facilitators to both the education and our practice with children experiencing homelessness. We discussed several common systems that are barriers and provided some description based on examples from practice and the literature on the topic. This conceptual base was developed from using the background knowledge on homelessness combined with the directions from the major policy governing our practice.

Conclusion

Earlier in the book we reviewed the history of studies on homeless children and youth in order to understand how we have come to our current understanding and focus of the issue. After this, we looked at the scope of the issue and looked at why people became homeless. We went over the general impact of homelessness on academic, behavioral and mental health, and physical health. We tried to come to a theoretical understanding of homelessness in comparison to those housed but still experiencing homelessness. Our examination of the literature led us to question whether we could determine types of homeless experiences. This was followed by an overview of what it is like to experience homelessness. We then reviewed the major provisions of the McKinney-Vento Homeless Assistance Act that will influence our practice. After this we went over what the MVA means for our practice, how to assess it, and what the literature says about its effectiveness. Finally, we went over a practice mindset for us to take to our school-based practice. We should focus on addressing the barriers and facilitators present in our school at the macro levels as well as the ones present for each individual student we serve. Now that we have a solid understanding on the impact of homelessness on children, we need to make it meaningful for our school-based practice.

Our Practice with Those Experiencing Homelessness Is About Instability

Theoretically, it is the unease and stress that comes with the idea of residential instability that is the major factor that leads to poor outcomes. It is the not knowing about where one will sleep or find shelter that is the driving force behind the poor outcomes associated with residential instability. I think a good way to look at this is to relate it to riding a roller coaster. I used to get sick on roller coasters when I was a child. It was not really the ride itself, though it played a role, but all of the anxiety and worry and stress I built up waiting in line that was the real factor behind why I was getting sick. It is the same for our thoughts on homelessness and residential instability. It is not necessarily experiencing homelessness that primarily gives rise to bad outcomes for children and youth experiencing homelessness, though the experience has its risk factors, but it is in the unease of an overall unstable and precarious housing situation that is the main reason why homeless and impoverished kids have the problems they do.

What Does This All Mean for Our Practice?

Now that we have a basic understanding of the definition of homelessness, a practice approach, the MVA, the MVA in practice, and a brief overview of the literature on homelessness, we should take some time to summarize what this all means for our practice. This final section will be a brief rundown of the important information we should know as we practice with homeless children and youth.

Homelessness Is a Complex Issue

Homelessness is a complicated experience, with many different factors that can impact outcomes. The term *homeless* is a bit of a misnomer—people can actually have shelter inside of a house, but they may still be considered homeless. There are many different ways a child could be considered homeless: staying in a homeless shelter, living on the streets, living in an abandoned building, or temporarily living with friends or relatives. Each would allow a child to be eligible for services. Because of this, we need to remember that homelessness is an experience, meaning that there are many different factors that can help or our practice. Ecological-systems theory provides a good method for us to organize all of the different circumstances and elements in a homeless child's life that may impact outcomes. As we practice, we should keep an eye on the different structural and individual systems that will influence our practice. Furthermore, we need to understand that impacting one system will undoubtedly have an impact on other systems. What we are able to accomplish in the school will impact a homeless child's life outside of school, even though we may not be able to directly address certain systems outside of our control.

Homelessness Is a Period of Instability

We can characterize homelessness as a period of unexpected transience, meaning that homeless children move from housing situations, and thus

---

education situations, often and without warning. Unplanned school mobility is considered one of the major reasons why homeless children struggle academically. When a child misses school unexpectedly, it leads to increased absences, difficulties in diagnosing developmental disabilities, and prevents children from forming any attachment to the school. In addition, transience is in all facets of a homeless child's life: with friends, family, housing situations. Homelessness is a socially isolating experience. Shelters are usually separate from other housing units, homeless children have to make new friends every time they move, and often they have to get used to new school routines. Transience is an important issue we must address in practice.

Homeless Children and Youth Lack the Basic Tools to Succeed

Homeless children often lack the basic means to be successful in school. Hunger and health problems are major issues homeless children and youth experience. In addition, they may not have the necessary supplies or space to complete assignments. They may have many barriers to success that we will need to address. Because of this, we should take a barrier and facilitator approach and mindset in our practice with homeless children and youth. We need to identify what prevents success, barriers, and use those factors that facilitate success. Furthermore, barriers and facilitators share an inverse relationship. What is not preventing success for homeless children and youth is in turn helping these students achieve their goals.

Attendance

Children and youth experiencing homelessness often miss an inordinate amount of school days. This is thought to stem from transience and unplanned school mobility, but a lack of resources such as transportation may also lead to why homeless children have poor attendance. Poor attendance is linked to many poor academic outcomes such as lower standardized test scores, grade retention, and dropout. However, attendance is one of the few academic outcomes that schools can directly address and many of our interventions will center on getting homeless students in school. Much of our practice will focus on providing homeless children and youth equal educational opportunities.

The MVA Is about Equal Opportunity

The MVA is a powerful policy that governs much of our practice with children and youth experiencing homelessness. The educational purpose of the policy is to provide equal educational opportunities for homeless children. To do this, the policy provides mandates that can be categorized in three areas: preparation, accessibility, and collaboration. According to the MVA, states and schools must be ready for the needs homeless children may have as they pursue education. Next, schools must make themselves accessible to homeless children and youth. This means that certain administrative requirements for school enrollment should be waived. The policy dictates that homeless children and youth must be enrolled immediately and maintain enrollment even if experiencing homelessness takes a child outside of school geographical boundaries. This is done to address transience and provide some semblance of stability. Finally, the MVA requires schools to collaborate with families and outside agencies to help homeless children. The legislation requires schools to not only search for homeless children, but also provide information that improves awareness of educational rights. While we may not know the extent to which the MVA is successful in providing equal educational opportunity, we do know that the policy has shaped how we practice with homeless children and the tasks we undertake.

Long-Term Impact of Homelessness Is Relatively Unknown

The influence of the MVA on practice is often discussed in the literature with mostly positive regard. However, we have few quantitative examinations of whether the MVA can be considered a success. Part of this is due to a lack of measurement on what we mean when we say that we are providing equal educational opportunity, tracking outcomes beyond number of children served, or poor data collection in general. Even fewer are longitudinal studies of how the MVA can impact outcomes long-term. In addition, there are few studies that document the long-term impact of experiencing homelessness. We can however, logic some of this out. For example, if homelessness leads to poor academic outcomes, such as a dramatically increased risk for dropout, then children who experience homelessness are at high risk of low employment opportunities and poverty from not having a high school diploma.

Conclusion

I hope this book was helpful. Over the course of the chapters, we have discussed many different topics and how they relate to our school-based practice. We have discussed a practice approach by viewing the homeless situation as various systems that serve as either barriers or facilitators to our practice. We

---

have a solid overview of the policy that governs our practice and provides mandates to uphold the right to equal education for homeless youth. We now also have a good understanding of the complex body of literature on the issue. Homelessness is an issue that is not going away any time soon. Our schools must be ready for this growing issue, and often the responsibility of helping homeless children and youth obtain equal educational opportunities falls to us as school social workers and related-services personnel. We need to make sure that we are adequately prepared and knowledgeable about this complex issue.

Practice Takeaways

- Viewing homelessness as a series of barriers or facilitators can help us with the complexity of the issue.
- We should strive to view our practice with homeless children and youth in the context of barriers and facilitators.
- Barriers are anything that hinders practice.
- Facilitators are anything that helps practice.
- What does not facilitate is a barrier and vice versa.
- We can change barriers into facilitators.
- Systems theory can help us identify barriers and facilitators.

References

Abell, N., Springer, D., & Kamata, A. (2009). *Developing and validating rapid assessment instruments*. New York: Oxford University Press.

Alexander, K., Entwisle, D., & Horsey, C. (1997). From first grade forward: Early foundations of high school dropout. *Sociology of Education, 70,* 87–107.

Allen-Meares, P. (2010). *Social work services in schools* (6th ed). Boston: Pearson.

Altshuler, S. (2003). From barriers to successful collaboration: Public schools and child welfare working together. *Social Work, 48,* 52–62.

Anderson, M. D. (2011). Special Schools for Homeless Students Bursting at the Seams. (cover story). *Education Week, 30,* 1.

Anooshian, L. (2003). Social isolation and rejection of homeless children. *Journal of Children & Poverty, 9,* 115–134.

Anooshian, L. (2005). Violence and aggression in the lives of homeless children. *Journal of Family Violence, 20,* 373–387.

Baggerly, J. (2003). Child-centered play therapy with children who are homeless: Perspective and procedures. *International Journal of Play Therapy, 12,* 87–106.

Banyard, V. (1995). "Taking another route": Daily survival narratives from mothers who are homeless. *American Journal of Community Psychology, 23,* 871–890.

Barrow, S., & Laborde, N. (2008). Invisible mothers: Parenting by homeless women separated from their children. *Gender Issues, 25,* 157–172.

Barrow, S., & Lawinski, T. (2009). Contexts of mother-child separations in homeless families. *Analyses of Social Issues and Public Policy, 9,* 157–176.

Barwick, M., & Siegel, L. (1996). Learning difficulties in adolescent clients of a shelter for runaway and homeless street youths. *Journal of Research on Adolescence, 6,* 649–670.

Bassuk, E. et al. (1996). The characteristics and needs of sheltered homeless and low-income housed mothers. *JAMA: The Journal of the American Medical Association, 276,* 640–646.

Bassuk, E. et al. (1997). Homelessness in female-headed families: Childhood and adult risk and protective factors. *American Journal of Publich Health, 87,* 241–248.

Berliner, D. (2009). *Poverty and potential: Out-of-school factors and school success*. Boulder, CO: Education and the Public Interest Center & Education Policy Research Unit.

Bertrand, J., Hardee, K., Magnani, R., & Angle, M. (1995). Access, quality of care and medical barriers in family planning programs. *International Family Planning Perspectives, 21,* 64–74.

Biggar, H. (2001). Homeless children and education: An evaluation of the Stewart B. McKinney Homeless Assistance Act. *Children and Youth Services Review, 23,* 941–969.

Bowman, D., & Barksdale, K. (2004). *Increasing school stability for students experiencing homelessness: Overcoming challenges to providing transportation to the school of origin*. Greensboro, NC: National Center for Homeless Education at SERVE.

Buckner, J. (2008). Understanding the impact of homelessness on children: Challenges and future research directions. *American Behavioral Scientist, 51*, 721–736.

Buckner, J., Bassuk, E., & Weinreb, L. (2001). Predictors of academic achievement among homeless and low-income housed children. *Journal of School Psychology, 39*, 45–69.

Burt, M. (2003). Chronic homelessness: Emergence of a public policy. *Fordham Urban Law Journal, XXX*, 1267–1279.

Canfield, J. (2014). Examining barriers to school social work practice with homeless children. *Children & Schools, 36*, 165–173.

Canfield, J., Teasley, M., Abell, N., & Randolph, K. (2012). Validating a McKinney-Vento Act Implementation Scale. *Research on Social Work Practice, 22*, 410–419.

Cauce, A., et al. (2000). The characteristics and mental health of homeless adolescents: Age and gender differences. *Journal of Emotional and Behavioral Disorders, 8*, 230–239.

Chambers, C., et al. (2014). Factors associated with poor mental health status among homeless women with and without dependent children. *Community Mental Health Journal, 50*, 553–559.

Congressional Research Service. (2005). Homelessness: Recent statistics, targeted federal programs, and recent legislation. Washington, DC: Library of Congress.

Cowal, K., Shinn, M., Weitzman, B., Stojanovic, D., & Labay, L. (2002). Mother-child separations among homeless and housed families receiving public assistance in New York City. *American Journal of Community Psychology, 30*, 711–730.

Culhane, D., Metraux, S., Park, J., Schretzman, M., & Valente, J. (2007). Testing a typology of family homelessness based on patterns of public shelter utilization in four U.S. jurisdictions: Implications for policy and program planning. *Housing Policy Debate, 18*, 1–28.

Culhane, J., Webb, D., Grim, S., Metraux, S., & Culhane, D. (2003). Prevalence of child welfare services involvement among homeless and low-income mothers: A five-year birth cohort study. *Journal of Sociology and Social Welfare, XXX*, 79–95.

Cutuli, J., Herbers, J., Rinaldi, M., Masten, A., & Oberg, C. (2010). Asthma and behavior in homeless 4 to 7 year-olds. *Pediatrics, 125*, 145–151.

Danesco, E., & Holden, E. (1998). Are there different types of homeless families? A typology of homeless families based on cluster analysis. *Family Relations, 47*, 159–165.

Daskal, J. (1998). *In search of shelter: The growing shortage of affordable rental housing*. Washington, DC: Center on Budget and Policy Priorities.

Davey, T., Penuel, W., Allison-Tant, E., & Rosner, A. (2000). The HERO Program: A case for school social work services. *Social Work in Education, 22*, 177–190.

Di Santo, A. (2012). Promoting preschool literacy: A family literacy program for homeless mothers and their children. *Childhood Education, 88*, 232–240.

DiMarco, Huff, M., Kinion, E., & Kendra, M. (2009). The pediatric nurse practitioner's role in reducing oral health disparities in homeless children. *Journal of Pediatric Health Care, 23*, 109–116.

Dotson, H. (2011). Homeless women, parents, and children: A triangulation approach analyzing factors influencing homelessness and child separation. *Journal of Poverty, 15*, 241–258.

Douglass, A. (1996). Rethinking the effects of homelessness on children: Resiliency and Competency. *Child Welfare, LXXV*, 741–751.

Duffield, B., & Lovell, P. (2008). *The economic crisis hits home: The unfolding increase in child & Youth Homelessness.* Washington, DC: National Association for the Education of Homeless Children and Youth.

Duval, D., & Vincent, N. (2009). Affect regulation of homeless youth once in the child welfare system. *Child Adolescent Social Work, 26,* 155–173.

Dworak-Fisher, S. (2009). Educational stability for students without homes: Realizing the promise of McKinney-Vento. *Journal of Poverty Law and Policy, 42,* 542–550.

Epstein, J., & Sheldon, S. (2002). Present and accounted for: Improving student attendance through family and community involvement. *The Journal of Educational Research, 95,* 308–318.

Fantuzzo, J., & Perlman, S. (2007). The unique impact of out of home placement and the mediating effects of child maltreatment and homelessness on early school success. *Children and Youth Services Review, 29,* 941–960.

Fantuzzo, J., LeBoeuf, W., Brumley, B., & Perlman, S. (2013). A population-based inquiry of homeless episode characteristics and early educational well-being. *Children and Youth Services Review, 35,* 966–972.

Fierman, A., et al. (1991). Growth delay in homeless children. *Pediatrics, 88,* 918–925.

Fredudenberger, H., & Torkelsen, S. (1984). Beyond the interpersonal: A systems model of the therapeutic care for homeless children and youth. *Psychotherapy, 21,* 132–140.

Gewirtz, A., Hart-Shegos, E., & Medhanie, A. (2008). Psychosocial status of homeless children and youth in family supportive housing, *American Behavioral Scientist, 51,* 810–823.

Glassman, M., Karno, D., & Erdem, G. (2010). The problems and barriers of RHYA as social policy. *Children and Youth Service Review, 32,* 798–806.

Grant, R., Bowen, S., McLean, D., Berman, D., Redlener, K., & Redlener, I. (2007). Asthma among homeless children in New York City: An update. *American Journal of Public Health, 97,* 448–450.

Groton, D., Teasley, M., & Canfield, J. (2013). Working with Homeless School Children: Barriers to School Social Work Practice. *School Social Work Journal, 37,* 37–51.

Gully, K., Koller, S., & Ainsworth, A. (2001). Exposure of homeless children to family violence: An adverse effect beyond alternative explanations. *Journal of Emotional Abuse, 2,* 5–18.

Haber, M., & Toro, P. (2004). Homelessness among families, children, and adolescents: An ecological-developmental perspective. *Clinical Child and Family Psychology Review, 7,* 123–164.

Hamann, S., Mooney, K., & Vrooman, C. (2002). *McKinney-Vento homeless education: Draft of proposed standards and indicators of quality McKinney-Vento programs.* Greensboro, NC: National Center for Homeless Education.

Harley, D. (2011). Perceptions of Hope and Hopelessness among Low-Income African American Adolescents. (Electronic Thesis or Dissertation). Retrieved from https://etd.ohiolink.edu/

Harley, D. (In Press). Perceptions of hopelessness among low-income African American adolescents through the lens of photovoice. *Journal of Ethnic & Cultural Diversity in Social Work.*

Hendricks, G., & Barkley, W. (2012). Necessary, but not sufficient: The McKinney–Vento Act and academic achievement in North Carolina. *Children & Schools, 34,* 179–185.

Herbers, J., et al. (2011). Direct and indirect effects of parenting on the academic functioning of young homeless children. *Early Education and Development, 22,* 77–104.

Herrington, D., Kidd-Herrington, K., & Kritsonis, M. (2006). Coming to terms with No Child Left Behind: Learning to teach the invisible children. *National Forum on Special Education Journal, 18,* 1–7.

Hicks-Coolick, A., Burnside, Eaton, P., & Peters, A. (2003). Homeless children: Needs and services. *Child & Youth Care Forum, 32,* 197–210.

Himmelstein, D., Warren, E., & Woolhandler, S. (2005). Illness and injury as contributors to bankruptcy. *Health Affairs: The Policy Journal of the Health Sphere.* Retrieved from http://www.healthaffairs.org/ or http://ssrn.com/abstractD664565

Hodgson, K., Shelton, K., van den Bree, M., & Los, F. (2013). Psychopathology in young people experiencing homelessness: A systematic review. *American Journal of Public Health, 103,* e24–e37.

Huntington, N., Buckner, J., & Bassuk, E. (2008). Adaptation in homeless children: An empirical examination using cluster analysis. *American Behavioral Scientist, 51,* 737–755.

James, B., & Lopez, P. (2003). Transporting homeless students to increase stability: A case study of two Texas districts. *The Journal of Negro Education, 72,* 126–140.

Johnson, R., Rew, L., & Sternglanz, R. (2006). The relationship between childhood sexual abuse and sexual health practices of homeless adolescent. *Adolescence, 41,* 221–234.

Jozefowicz-Simbeni, D., & Israel, N. (2006). Services to homeless students and families: The McKinney-Vento Act and its implications for school social work practice. *Children & Schools, 28,* 37–44.

Julianelle, P., & Foscarinis, M. (2003). Responding to the school mobility of children and youth experiencing homelessness: The McKinney-Vento Act and beyond. *The Journal of Negro Education, 72,* 39–54.

Kennedy, A. (2007). Homelessness, violence exposure, and school participation among urban adolescent mothers. *Journal of Community Psychology, 35,* 639–654.

Kilmer, R., Cook, J., Crusto, C., Strater, K., & Haber, M. (2012). Understanding the ecology and development of children and families experiencing homelessness: Implications for practice, supportive services, and policy. *American Journal of Orthopsychiatry, 82,* 389–401.

Kim, J. (2013). Confronting invisibility: Early childhood pre-service teachers' beliefs toward homeless children. *Early Childhood Education Journal, 41,* 161–169.

Kuhn, R., & Culhane, D. (1998). Applying cluster analysis to test a typology of homelessness by pattern of shelter utilization: Results from the analysis of administrative data. *American Journal of Community Psychology, 26,* 207–232.

Larsen, C. (2002). Balancing the books: The Stewart B. McKinney Homeless Assistance Act and separate schools for homeless children in Arizona. *Arizona State Law Journal, 34,* 705–731.

Markward, M., & Biros, E. (2001). McKinney revisisted: Implications for school social work. *Children & Schools, 36,* 182–187.

Massat, C., Constable, R., McDonald, S., & Flynn, J. (2009). *School Social Work: Practice, Policy, and Research.* Chicago: Lyceum.

McAllister, W., Kuang, L., & Lennon, (2010). Typologizing temporality: Time-aggregated and time-patterned approaches to conceptualizing homelessness. *Social Service Review, 84,* 225–256.

Menke, E. (1998). The mental health of homeless school-aged children. *Journal of Child and Adolescent Psychiatric Nursing, 11,* 87–98.

Menke, E. (2000). Comparison of the stressors and coping behaviors of homeless, previously homeless, and homeless poor children. *Issues in Mental Health Nursing, 21,* 691–710.

Mickelson, R., & Yon, M. (1995). The motivation of homeless children. *The International Journal of Social Education, 9,* 28–45.

Miller, P. (2009a). An examination of the McKinney-Vento Act and its influences on homeless education situation. *Educational Policy, 20,* 1–27.

Miller, P. (2009b). Leadership practice in service of homeless students: An examination of community perceptions. *Urban Revue, 41,* 222–250.

Miller, P. (2011a). A critical analysis of the research on student homelessness. *Review of Educational Research, 81,* 308–337.

Miller, P. (2011b). Homeless education and social capital: An examination of school and community leaders. *Teachers College Record, 113,* 1067–1104.

Miliotis, D., Sesma, A., & Masten, A. (1999). Parenting as a protective process for school success in children from homeless families. *Early Education & Development, 10,* 111–133.

National Center for Homeless Education. (2011). *Education for homeless children and youth program: Data collection summary.* Washington, DC: Author.

National Center on Family Homelessness. (2009). *America's Youngest Outcasts: State Report Card on Child Homelessness.* Newton, MA: Author.

National Coalition for the Homeless. (2009, July). *How many people experience homelessness?* Washington, DC: Author. Retrieved from http://www.nationalhomeless.org/factsheets/How_Many.html

Nolan, J. R., Cole, T., Wroughton, J., Riffe, H. A., & Clayton-Code, K. P. (2013). Assessment of risk factors for truancy of children in grades K-12 using survival analysis. *Journal of At-Risk Issues, 17,* 23.

Nooe, R., & Patterson, D. (2010). The ecology of homelessness. *Journal of Human Behavior in the Social Environment, 20,* 105–152.

Nyamathi, A., Hudson, A., Greengold, B., & Leake, B. (2012). Characteristics of homeless youth who use cocaine and methamphetamine. *The American Journal on Addictions, 21,* 243–249.

O'Leary, S. (2001). Educating homeless children. *Georgetown Journal on Poverty Law & Policy, 8,* 513–518.

Panter-Brick, C. (2004). Homelessness, poverty, and risks to health: Beyond at-risk categorizations of street children. *Children's Geographies, 2,* 83–94.

Payne, M. (2014). *Modern social work theory* (4th ed). Chicago: Lyceum Books, Inc.

Powers-Costello, B., & Swick, K. (2011). Transforming teacher constructs of children and families who are homeless. *Early Childhood Education Journal, 39,* 207–212.

Rafferty, Y., & Shinn, M., (1991). The impact of homelessness on children. *American Psychologist, 46,* 1170–1179.

Rafferty, Y., Shinn, M., & Weitzman, B. (2004). Academic achievement among formerly homeless adolescents and their continuously housed peers. *Journal of School Psychology*, *42*, 179–199.

Reed-Victor, E., & Pelco, L. (1999). Helping homeless students build resilience: What the school community can do. *Journal for a Just and Caring Education*, *5*, 51–71.

Richards, R., & Smith, C. (2007). Environmental, parental, and personal influences on food choice, access, and overweight status among homeless children. *Social Science & Medicine*, *65*, 1572–1583.

Roby, D. E. (2004). Research on school attendance and student achievement: A study of Ohio schools. *Educational Research Quarterly*, *28*, 3–16.

Rotheram-Borus, M., Koopman, C., & Ehrhardt, A. (1991). Homeless youths and HIV infection. *American Psychologist*, *46*, 1188–1197.

Rubin, A., & Babbie, E. (2010). *Essential research methods for social work* (2nd ed.). Belmont, CA: Brooks/Cole.

Rukmana, D. (2008). Where the homeless children and youth come from: A study of residential origins of the homeless in Miami Dade County, Florida. *Children and Youth Services Review*, *30*, 1009–1021.

Salomonsen-Sautel, S. et al. (2008). Correlates of substance use among homeless youths in eight cities. *The American Journal on Addictions*, *17*, 224–234.

Shinn, M., Schteingart, J., Williams, M., Carlin-Mathis, J., Bialo-Karagis, N., Becker-Klein, R., & Weitzman, B. (2008). Long-term associations of homelessness with children's well-being. *American Behavioral Scientist*, *51*, 789–809.

Sleath, B. et al. (2006). Literacy and perceived barriers to medication taking among homeless mothers and their children. *American Journal of Health-Systems Pharmacy*, *63*, 346–351.

Sosin, M. (2003). Explaining adult homelessness in the US by stratification or situation. *Journal of Community & Applied Social Psychology*, *13*, 91–104.

Spillane, J. (2000). Cognition and policy implementation: District policymakers and the reform of Mathematics education. *Cognition and Instruction*, *18*, 141–179.

Spillane, J., Reiser, B., & Reimer, T. (2002). Policy implementation and cognition: Reframing and refocusing implementation research. *Review of Education al Research*, *72*, 387–431.

Swick, K. (2003). The dynamics of families who are homeless: Implications for early childhood educators. *Childhood Education*, *80*, 116–120.

Teasley, M., Gourdine, R., & Canfield, J. (2010). Identifying perceived barriers and facilitators to culturally competent practice for school social workers. *School Social Work Journal*, *34*, 90–104.

The McKinney-Vento Homeless Assistance Act of 1987 42 U.S.C. § 11431, *et seq.* (2002).

Turner, F. (1996). *Social work treatment* (4th. ed.). New York: The Free Press.

Tyler, K. Whitbeck, L., Hoyt, D., & Cauce, A. (2004). Risk factors for secual victimization among male and female homeless and runaway youth. *Journal of Interpersonal Violence*, *19*, 503–520.

U.S. Conference of Mayors. (2005). *A status report on hunger and homelessness in America's cities 2005: A 24-city survey, December 2005*. Washington, DC: Author.

United States Department of Housing and Urban Development. (2007). Federal Definition of Homeless. Retrieved October 30, 2010 from http://www.hud.gov/homeless/definition.cfm.

Urban Institute. (2010). Residential instability and the McKinney-Vento homeless Children and Education Program: What we know, plus gaps in research. Washington DC: Author.

Van Doorn, L. (2010). Perceptions of time and space of (formerly) homeless people. *Journal of Human Behavior in the Social Environment, 20,* 218–238.

Walsh, T., & Douglas, H. (2009). Legal responses to child protection, poverty, and homelessness. *Journal of Social Welfare & Family Law, 31,* 133–146.

Weckstein, P. (2003). Accountability and student mobility under Title I of the No Child Left Behind Act. *The Journal of Negro Education, 72,* 117–125.

Weinger, S. (1998). Children living in poverty: Their perception of career opportunities. *Families in Society: The Journal of Contemporary Human Services, 79,* 320–330.

Willard, A., & Kulinna, P. (2012). Summer literacy intervention for homeless children living in transitional housing. *The Journal of At-Risk Issues, 17,* 15–22.

Wong, J., Salomon, A., Elliott, L., Tallarita, L., & Reed, S. (2004). The McKinney-Vento Homeless Assistance Act-education for homeless children and youths program: Turning good law into effective education. *Georgetown Journal on Poverty Law & Policy, 11,* 283–319.

Yousey, Y., Leake, J., Wdowik, M., & Janken, J. (2007). Education in a homeless shelter to improve the nutrition of young children. *Public Health Nursing, 24,* 249–255.

Zima, B., Bussing, R., Forness, S., & Benjamin, B. (1997). Sheltered homeless children: Their need for special education evaluations. *American Journal of Public Health, 87,* 236–240.eligibility and unmet

Zima, B., Wells, K., & Freeman, H. (1994). Emotional and behavioral problems nd severe academic delays among sheltered homeless children in Los Angeles County. *American Journal of Public Health, 84,* 260–264.

Index

physical well-being, 107–8, 109
Plyler v. Doe, 44
preparation provision in MVA
      implementation, 45–46,
      54, 113
psychometric studies, 69
psychosocial accessibility, 49, 52
public places, as housing option, 28
public schools. *See* schools

"red flag" indicators, 59
regular nighttime residence, 43
relationships, 83

school-based practitioners. *See also*
      school social workers, 10–11,
      44–45, 68
school mobility. *See also* transience,
      4, 96–97, 111–12
school nurses, 60–61, 63
schools. *See also* education
   abuse, suspicion of, 50
   accessibility, 54–55
   administrative accessibility
      and, 48
   administrators and, 58–59
   charter, 48
   collaboration with agencies
      outside of, 61
   communication between families
      and, 102
   conflicting purpose between
      outside entities and, 18
   enrollment personnel and, 59
   environment preparedness, 84
   gatekeepers to, 59
   immunization records, 48
   MVA and (*see* McKinney-Vento
      Homeless Assistance
      Act (MVA))
   skill-related public, 48
   teachers and, 56–58
   transition between, 101–2
school secretaries, 59, 62–63

school social workers
   abuse, suspicion of, 50
   attendance and, 97
   barriers for homeless children,
      4–5, 68
   case study, 85–89
   child homelessness
      identification, 55
   collaboration and, 49–50
   communication between school
      secretaries and, 59
   as conduit to outside world, 61
   equal education
      opportunities, 114
   homelessness in school-based
      practice, 37–38
   and MVA implementation,
      44–45, 68
   needs assessment and, 72
   practice setting for, 8
   role of, 10–11
school social work practice,
      10, 13–14, 44–45, 56, 78,
      90–91
sexual abuse, 30
shelters, 61, 112
shelter systems, 15
single female-headed households,
      17, 91, 102
skill-related public schools, 48
sobriety, 31
social isolation, 92
social rejection, 92
social support, 29–30
Stewart B. McKinney Act. *See also*
      McKinney-Vento Homeless
      Assistance Act (MVA), 15, 42
structural systems
   description of, 31–32
   example of, 32–37
substance abuse issues, 22, 30–31
systems theory. *See also*
      ecological-systems perspective,
      46, 82, 84, 114